Defining Moments

THE

CIVIL

WAR

DEFINING MOMENTS
THE
CIVIL
WAR

Michael Swift & George Grant

THUNDER BAY
P · R · E · S · S

San Diego, California

THUNDER BAY
P · R · E · S · S

Thunder Bay Press
An imprint of the Advantage Publishers Group
5880 Oberlin Drive, San Diego, CA 92121-4794
www.thunderbaybooks.com

All notations of errors or omissions should be addressed to Thunder Bay Press, Editorial Department, at the above address. All other correspondence (author inquiries, permissions) concerning the content of this book should be addressed to: TAJ Books, 27 Ferndown Gardens, Cobham, Surrey, UK, KT11 2BH, info@tajbooks.com.

ISBN 1-59223-435-6

Library of Congress Cataloging-in-Publication Data available upon request.

Printed in China
1 2 3 4 5 09 08 07 06 05

CONTENTS

Introduction

In 1860, the United States of America was still a young country; it was less than 90 years since the Declaration of Independence had seen the country throw off its colonial ties to Great Britain. It was also a country that was expanding rapidly as settlers moved westward from the eastern seaboard into the Midwest and beyond.

Following the Treaty of Paris of 1783, which settled the War of Independence, the form of the new nation was still not finalized. Within the original Thirteen Colonies of New England there was no definite agreement as to the nature of the post-colonial era. In each state there were those who argued for a federal structure and those who argued for the independence of each individual colony. On May 25, 1787, the Constitutional Convention opened in Philadelphia. For the next four months, the convention argued about the new constitution before agreeing, on September 17, to promote a federal structure. Each former colony had to then ratify the new constitution. The first state to ratify the constitution was Delaware on December 7, 1787; the last was Rhode Island on May 29, 1790. Apart from the original colonies, the United States also included the territories to the east of the Mississippi, such as Kentucky and Tennessee, which had been previously French, but ceded to Britain in 1763. These were only gradually to achieve statehood: Kentucky in 1792, Tennessee in 1796, Ohio in 1803, Mississippi in 1817, and Alabama in 1819.

Even after the War of Independence, there were areas—in particular the areas that were later to form the states of Michigan, Illinois, and Indiana— where the British claimed jurisdiction. These lands were only ceded to the United States in 1795 after the Jay Treaty. Known initially as the Northwest Territory, these regions were gradually carved into new states and the native Indian population subjugated.

The first half of the 19th century was the period of expansion, as the United States grew from its east coast beginnings to span the continent. First there was the Louisiana Purchase of 1803 when the Emperor Napoleon sold the region for $15 million. Next, the Mississippi delta was annexed from Spain in 1810 and 1812. This acquisition was followed in 1819 by Spain ceding three further territories: Florida, the acquisition of which was ratified by the United States in 1821; the area of Louisiana to the west of the Mississippi delta; and the southwestern part of the future state of Oklahoma. In the north, improved relations with the British saw the regularization of the U.S.–Canadian border in 1818 along the 49th parallel: Britain ceded the northern part of North Dakota and Minnesota and gained an area to the north on Montana in compensation. In 1842 the Webster-Ashburton Treaty with Britain regularized the border of Maine and Canada, seeing the U.S. expand to the north up to Fort Kent, and also the section of Minnesota along the coast of Lake Superior. The last U.S.– British territorial settlement concerned Oregon Country—the region which was to form the future states of Washington, Oregon, Idaho, and the western part of Montana—which had been jointly held by Britain and the U.S. since 1818 and which was transferred to U.S. sovereignty in 1846. Although the settlement was achieved peacefully, the dispute over this region—with the British fearing that the U.S. would seek jurisdiction as far north and the 54th parallel—was the closest that Britain and the U.S. came to war after 1812.

Further south, the largely English-speaking settlers of Texas revolted against their Mexican overlords in 1835, declaring the Texan Republic on March 2, 1836, with a constitution largely based upon that adopted by the U.S. at the end of the 18th century. War broke out between the settlers and the Mexican authorities, who were eager to see their powers restored. It was during this war that the famous battle at the Alamo took place, when a small rebel force held out against a numerically much larger Mexican army. The rebel forces had the advantage of holding a strong fortress against a largely conscript and untrained government army, but numbers in the end won the day for the Mexicans. Not all the rebels were killed in the battle; a number, including Davy Crockett, survived and were later executed. The defeat at the Alamo was followed by a massacre at Goliad of some 350 rebels. The Texan army under General Sam Houston redressed the balance, defeating the Mexicans on April 21, 1836, after which Texan independence was recognized.

The United States recognized Texan independence in July 1836 but, on August 25, 1837, turned down an initial approach for the new republic to join the Union. The "Lone Star Republic" was, however, only to have a short independent life; on December 29, 1845, Texas became the 28th state. Part of the territory was to form the eastern part of New Mexico while part became southwestern Kansas.

Zachary Taylor (1784-1850) became the 12th President of the United States.

This led to a border war with Mexico. The United States claimed the border should now be formed by the Rio Grande and not the Nueces River, which had been regarded as the border up until that point. The U.S. authorities also objected to a Mexican prohibition on the further migration of English-speaking settlers in California. On March 8, 1846, U.S. forces led by General Zachary Taylor crossed the Nueces into the disputed territory between that river and the Rio Grande. Following the death of 11 Americans on April 25, 1846, the U.S. declared war on Mexico on May 11, invading north California, where U.S. settlers revolted at Sonoma (the Bear Flag Revolt of June 14, 1846), just to the north of San Francisco, along the Gila River. Victories at Monterrey (September 21–24, 1846), San Gabriel (January 8, 1847), Buena Vista (February 22/23, 1847), and Chapultepec (September 13, 1847) saw U.S. forces occupy many of the major Mexican cities, including Mexico City itself, San Francisco, Santa Barbara, Santa Fe, Albuquerque, and Veracruz. The war was settled by the Treaty of Guadalupe Hidalgo, which became effective on July 4, 1848; for the price of $15 million, the U.S. acquired California and New Mexico, and the Mexican authorities also waived all claims on Texas. The final border settlement in this region came with the Gadsden Purchase of 1852, when the U.S. acquired the southernmost parts of New Mexico and Arizona.

Reynold's political map of the United States, designed to exhibit the comparative area of the free and slave states and the territory open to slavery or freedom by the repeal of the Missouri Compromise.

Slavery

The transatlantic slave trade reached its peak in the late 18th century, as the colonial masters of the Caribbean islands and North America—primarily the British and French—imported vast numbers of black Africans to work in the plantations, initially to farm tobacco and sugar but increasingly cotton as well.

While the trade was hugely profitable, there was a significant trend toward abolition. Denmark made participation in the slave trade illegal by in 1792; the U.S. did the same two years later. Theoretically, this meant that no new slaves would be imported into the U.S. after that date, although it did not free those slaves already present nor their children and successive generations. In Britain, people such as William Wilberforce actively campaigned for abolition. In 1807 British involvement in the trade was made illegal. In 1834 slavery within British possessions in the Caribbean was also made illegal. However, in the U.S., particularly in the south, slavery remained an essential part of the economic structure of the society and, as the U.S. expanded westward into, for example, Texas, so the slave-owning regions grew.

Slavery lasted in the south because of economic factors, in particular the needs of the plantation owners—always a minority of the white population—for a source of cheap labor. However, poor-quality land and intensive farming had resulted in the degradation of much of the land in the traditional slave-owning areas to the north, with the result that, by the outbreak of the Civil War in 1861, these areas were by no means guaranteed to support the retention of slavery.

The pro-slavery lobby in the south—fearful in particular after Nat Turner's rising in Southampton County, Virginia, on August 22, 1831, when some 60 whites were massacred in the last black rebellion before the Civil War—was increasingly active in promoting retention. The were three main strands to the pro-slavery lobby: first, that slavery was the natural status of the black population in that it was inferior to the white population in intellect; second, that slavery was permitted by the Bible and there was nothing contradictory between it and Christianity; and finally, that slavery offered a form of safe existence for a race that was otherwise incapable of looking after itself. These beliefs were added to later by those who drew unfavorable comparison between the free labor of the north, with its alleged insecurity, and slavery, which was claimed to offer a lifetime of support.

At the outbreak of the Civil War in 1861, the black slave population in the south numbered some four million, representing more than half of the population in many of the southern states. In addition to these, there were also "free" blacks in both the north and the south, although the rights that these enjoyed were severely constrained. In terms of resistance from the slave population, the period after Turner's rising in 1831 was marked by increased passive resistance and by large numbers escaping to the north, to Canada, and to the islands of the Caribbean.

A large number of black fugitives also fought alongside the Indians in the Second Seminole War of 1835–42.

Secession looms

The constitution adopted by the founding fathers gave the U.S. no federal rights over slavery and no powers to abolish it where it existed under state laws. Moreover, the constitution had also not predetermined the position of future states seeking admission to the Union—a critical factor considering the expansion of the country during the first half of the 19th century—although, in theory, Congress had the power to request abolition from those states seeking admission. However, when in 1819–20, Congress had sought to exercise this power, controversy had resulted and led to the so-called Missouri Compromise, in which it was agreed that land to the south of the 36° 30' line would be permitted to retain slavery on entering the Union. This compromise lasted for over 25 years until the question of incorporating the land wrought from the Mexicans arose.

Theoretically, under the Missouri Compromise, the area that would later form Texas, New Mexico, and California all fell to the south of the line and this would, undoubtedly, have shifted the national balance in favor of the pro-slavery states. The first effort to resolve this came in August 1846 when Representative David Wilmot of Pennsylvania proposed an amendment that would bar slavery from all territory acquired from Mexico by the simple means of ensuring that the new territories would be white-only. Another proposal, made by Senator Lewis Cass of Michigan, was that the question of slavery should be left to the new settlers. The thorny question remained unresolved by the presidential election of 1848, which saw Zachary Taylor elected. He sought to get round the issue by admitting both California and New Mexico immediately as states. This, however, upset the south who saw it as an attempt to weaken the pro-slavery lobby.

In June 1850, representatives of the southern states met at Nashville, Tennessee, to formulate a common position. President Taylor rejected compromise but the position changed dramatically in July 1850 when he died and was replaced by the more amenable Millard Fillmore. The passage of a new compromise was also aided by the fact that, instead of Congress voting on a single measure, the proposal was broken down into separate sections with the result that the opposition to individual parts did not result in the whole being lost. The result of the compromise was to see the slave trade abolished in Washington, D.C.; California admitted as a free state; the enactment of a new and stronger Fugitive Law; and votes to take place in both New Mexico and Utah to determine whether these new territories would be slave free or not.

This compromise resulted in a further brief period of stability but in January 1854, Senator Stephen Douglas of Illinois, proposed organizing the territory to the west of Missouri—an area now occupied by the states of Kansas and Nebraska. Theoretically this territory was to the north of the 36° 10' line and so would be free; however, in Douglas' proposed act both territories would be permitted to vote on whether to permit slavery. Such a proposal was widely condemned in the north and resulted in the effective demise of the old Whig party, which was replaced by a new political force—the Republican Party—with its up and coming young star, Abraham Lincoln.

By the time of the presidential election of 1856, the new Republican Party was well supported. Its candidate, John C. Frémont, did well in the north, but crucially, less well in the south where the anti-Democratic vote was split between him and Millard Fillmore. This meant that Democrat James Buchanan secured office, but the success of the Republicans in the north indicated that they stood every chance of winning four years later.

Shortly after Buchanan's inauguration, one of the keystones of the status quo was destroyed when the Supreme Court ruled in the case of Dred and Harriet Scott—slaves who lived in the "free" state of Wisconsin—when their master died. The ruling meant that the Missouri Compromise was effectively unconstitutional, which enraged the anti-slavery movement in the north, who called the decision "a wicked and false judgement," pointing to the number of pro-slavery southern judges on the Supreme Court as being evidence of bias.

During the second half of the 1850s, tension continued to rise. On May 22, 1856, for example, Representative Clayton Brooks of South Carolina entered the Senate where he assaulted Senator Charles Sumner of Massachusetts over Sumner's opposition to slavery. The injuries that Sumner sustained kept him out of politics for three years. The Lecompton Controversy saw an attempt during 1858 to create a constitution for the new state of Kansas that would have allowed the ownership of slaves. The proposed constitution was rejected in Congress.

Southern fears over the anti-slavery movement were increased both by anti-slavery books—such as Hinton Rowan Helper's The Impending Crisis of the South that encouraged the poor whites in the south to take action against the plantation owners—and also by physical events, such as John Brown's raid on Harper's Ferry. The South's worst nightmare took place in 1860 with the election of Abraham Lincoln as president. There could be no doubt now: slavery was under real threat and the only means to avoid its loss was secession. The road to the Civil War was wide open.

Draft of Lincoln's instructions to Major Robert Anderson, commander of Fort Sumter, April 4, 1861. In it Lincoln says that he has "confidence that you will act as a patriot and a soldier under all circumstances."

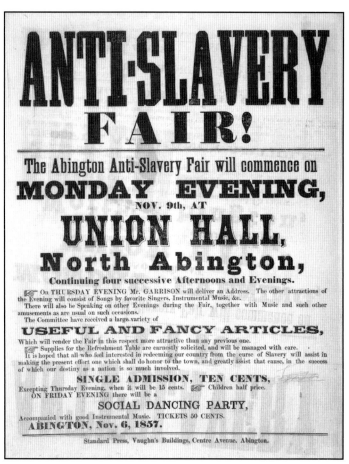

Slavery was the main reason that the differences between North and South led to war: most other issues could have been sorted out politically. The financial dependence of the southern states on slave labor, and the antagonism that slavery aroused, meant that war was almost inevitable.

RHODE ISLAND ABOLISHES SLAVERY 1774

During the 18th century vast numbers of Africans were shipped across the Atlantic to become slaves on the sugar and cotton plantations of North America and the Caribbean. Much of this trade was controlled by the British, whose ships sailed from Bristol and other ports to West Africa loaded with manufactured goods which were bartered for slaves. This human cargo crossed the Atlantic to the New World, where the surviving slaves were sold and replaced as cargo by tobacco, sugar, and cotton, materials required back in Europe.

The so-called "Triangular Trade" was one of the bedrocks of British prosperity in the period and many of the wealthiest families owed much to their involvement with the profits from the trade. By the end of the century, however, there was increasing opposition to the slave trade and movements for its abolition were established. Many of the most prominent individuals in North America, such as George Washington, were personally opposed to slavery, although there was little co-ordination amongst these individuals to obtain abolition. Often these individuals—again, as George Washington—were to free their slaves in their wills, but this affected a fraction of the estimated 250,000 slaves that existed within the Thirteen Colonies before Independence.

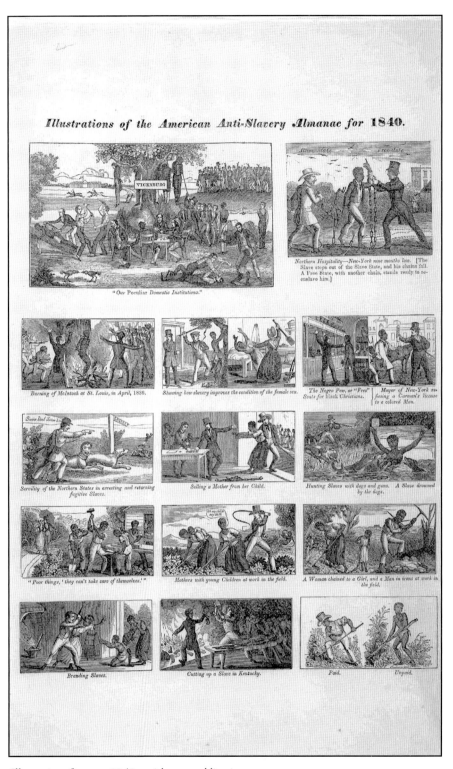

Illustrations from an 1840 antislavery publication.

Rhode Island, one of the original Thirteen Colonies that constituted the British territories, had a tradition of religious toleration—many of the abolitionists held strong religious beliefs—and it was here in 1774 that slavery was first abolished in North America. As the smallest of the colonies (and the future smallest state), Rhode Island was not a major center of slave-owning; however, as one of the northern colonies, it set a precedent that was to be followed by others, gradually creating the divide between the abolitionist north and the slave-owning south.

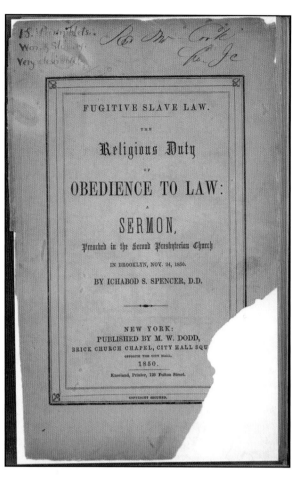

The Fugitive Slave Act of 1850 was part of a compromise that saw California admitted to the Union as a "free" state. It aroused great anger in the North and did nothing to curtail the activities of the Underground Railway.

CONGRESS AND THE FUGITIVE SLAVE LAW 1850

The first Fugitive Slave Law had been passed in 1793, but by the middle of the 19th century, with the U.S. expanding rapidly to the west and south, the balance between the abolitionist and pro-slavery states was in danger of fracture. As part of a settlement to allow for the incorporation of California, Texas, New Mexico, and Utah into the Union—although with differing constitutional arrangements—it was agreed that a new, and much stricter, Fugitive Slave Law would be enacted to replace the earlier act.

As part of the compromise, slavery was abolished in the District of Columbia but this positive move was countered by the more draconian elements within the revised Fugitive Slave Law. Under the revised act, the rights of the accused were much reduced: suspected fugitives were denied a trial by jury as well as the right to testify on their own behalf. The consequence of this was that there were no safeguards against false identification and the kidnapping of legally free blacks.

The new act was opposed by many of the leading abolitionists, although many were equally opposed to violence, such as William Lloyd Garrison (who had founded the journal Liberator in 1831 and was one

This is a portrait of fugitive slave Anthony Burns, whose arrest and trial in Boston under the provisions of the Fugitive Slave Act of 1850, incited riots and protests by white and black antislavery campaigners.

of the leading journalists of the period). Others, however, saw in the new act as an erosion of the route to abolition through non-violence. One of the most notable black leaders and orators of the abolition movement— Frederick Douglass who had escaped from Maryland—commented in October 1850, "The only way to make the Fugitive Slave Law a dead letter is to make half a dozen or more dead kidnappers."

As during the War of Independence, Boston was a center of opposition to the new act. Here, noted orator Endell Phillips, who had been inspired by Garrison's opposition to join the campaign, was prominent in ensuring that the issue of slavery remained at the forefront of debate. However, despite the opposition, the compromise was seen as a means of ensuring that the country did not fracture.

Harpers Ferry, on the confluence of the Potomac and the Shenandoah, was the site of the Federal arsenal that John Brown of Kansas attempted to take. He wanted the weapons to help start a slave insurrection.

John Brown and Harpers Ferry October 1859

Although the compromise led to a period of relative peace, tensions about slavery were never far from the surface. One of the most notable figures during the period between the compromise and the election of Lincoln as president was John Brown (1800–59). He first came to prominence in May 1856 during the Bleeding Kansas upheaval when the territory, which did not join the Union until 1861, was fought over by abolitionists and pro-slavers. In response to an attack by pro-slavers on the town of Lawrence, Brown murdered five pro-slavery men.

Three years later, he tried again to spark revolution amongst the slaves themselves. His plan was to seize weapons, march into the south, raise a rebel slave army, and retreat into the Appalachian Mountains from where his forces would launch raids upon the slave-owning states. Despite the irrationality of the plan, Brown raised money to fund it and, on October 16, 1859, he and 18 followers captured the federal arsenal at Harpers Ferry, located on the upper Potomac, from where he issued a proclamation to the slaves.

The federal authorities acted quickly; the army of Virginia, under Robert E. Lee, rapidly forced Brown and his supporters to surrender. Brown was tried at Richmond, Virginia, and executed by hanging as were six of his followers. The party that executed him, drawn from the Virginia Military Academy, was commanded by one of the great future figures of the Confederate army, "Stonewall" Jackson. Brown, in spite of his many faults, was an inspiration to many abolitionists, for whom the words in the song about his death—"But his soul goes marching on"—epitomized the struggle for emancipation.

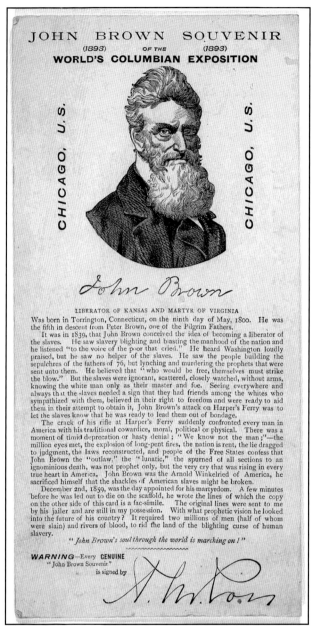

Immortalized in song and souvenirs, John Brown's actions polarized opinion: to the South it fostered the idea of the unthinkable: slave insurrection facilitated by the North. In the North, Brown was seen as a martyr by many.

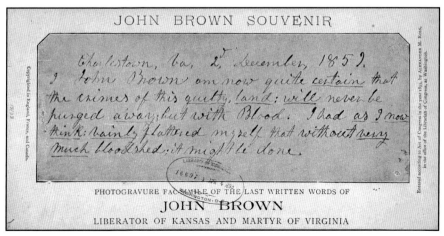

John Brown's last words.

Portrait of Abraham Lincoln.

ABRAHAM LINCOLN ELECTED PRESIDENT 1860

Born in 1809, the son of a poor and illiterate farming family in a Kentucky township, Abraham Lincoln spent much of early life in Indiana, where his family moved in 1816 and where he received his limited education. The family moved to Illinois in 1831, and Lincoln ran a store, served as postmaster, and studied law in New Salem. He was admitted to the Bar in 1836 before moving to Springfield, Illinois.

Active, at this time, as a Democrat politician, he served four terms in the State Legislature and also spent a short period in Congress (1847–49), before changing to the Republican party in 1856 as a result of his belief that slavery was irreconcilable with freedom and equality. He stood for the Senate in 1858 against Stephen Douglas (a supporter of slavery) but lost. His reputation, however, saw him selected as the Republican candidate for President in 1860, although he was helped by the fact that the Republican Convention was held in Chicago and that William Henry Seward, his main opponent for the nomination, was regarded as too extreme an abolitionist as well as too sympathetic to immigrants and Catholics.

The Democrats were hopelessly divided, with three candidates—including Senator Douglas—representing various sections of the party. In the event, Lincoln triumphed, but obtained only 39% of the popular vote; while he won most of the northern and western states, he failed to capture a single state in the south. He became the 16th President of the United States—and, at 6ft 4in one of the tallest—following his inauguration in 1861, but over a severely divided nation. Even before his entry into office, the south was already plotting to secede.

William H. Seward was Lincoln's opponent for the Republican nomination in the 1860 presidential elections and became Secretary of State in Lincoln's government.

Portrait of Lincoln's Vice President — Hannibal Hamlin.

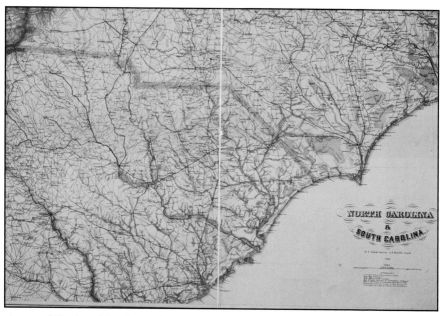

A map of North and South Carolina: both would secede from the Union—the south on December 20, 1860; the north after the fall of Fort Sumter.

THE SOUTH SECEDES JANUARY 1861

Lincoln's electoral victory ensured that there was little chance of compromise; indeed, before his inauguration in March, while Democrat James Buchanan retained office, the first secessions took place. At the forefront of the pro-slavery states, South Carolina voted to withdraw from the Union on December 20, 1860. The rationale behind the decision was that, just as each individual state had voted in convention to join the Union, so a vote in a similar body could see the individual state withdraw. For a brief period, other southern states did not act so precipitously, hoping that some form of compromise could still be found. However, during January 1861, a further six southern states—Alabama, Mississippi, Florida, Georgia, Louisiana, and Texas—also voted to secede. So far, all the secessionist states were those from the deep south. The more northerly pro-slavery states—North Carolina, Virginia, Arkansas, and Tennessee—remained within the Union; indeed, they would not actually secede until after the fall of Fort Sumter.

On February 4, 1861, delegates from the seven secessionist states met in a convention at Montgomery in Alabama in order to establish the Confederate States of America and to agree a new constitution. At the convention, the moderates within the pro-slavery states held sway and many of the more extreme motions—such as a demand for the restoration of the transatlantic slave trade with Africa—were successfully resisted. The draft constitution, officially issued on March 11, 1861, was in most respects very similar to the original constitution of the U.S., save for the fact that it adopted a pro-southern interpretation of the contentious clauses within the original contract and also enshrined the position of slavery. The convention also selected Jefferson Davis and Alexander H. Stephens as provisional President and Vice-President respectively.

Portrait of Confederate Vice President Alexander Stephens.

Despite the secession and the adoption of the Confederate constitution there were still those in both camps that sought to effect a compromise. In James Buchanan, however, there was a weak, lame-dog, President whose ineffectiveness in the face of the growing crisis made the position worse. All hope for preventing the secession disappeared when, at his inauguration on March 4, 1861, Lincoln's speech rejected compromise over slavery.

Personnel of the 1862 Confederate Congress.

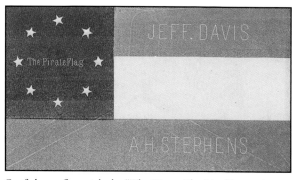

Confederate flag with the "The Pirate Flag" in blue section and Davis and Stephens on red bars.

The Confederate Secretary of State Robert M. T. Hunter.

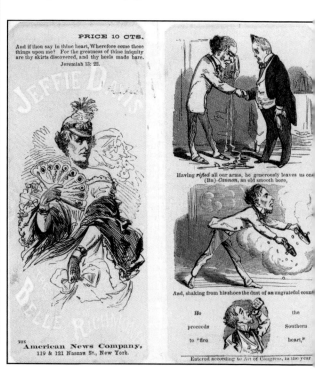

A poster from the first national bank Gainesville, Georgia on the Confederate half century memorial.

"Jeffie Davis the belle of Richmond." The American News Company 1865.

The "White House of the Confederacy," Jefferson Davis' house in Richmond, Va.

THE SOUTH CREATES A GOVERNMENT FEBRUARY 1861

The constitution of the Confederate states, issued on March 11, 1861, but agreed earlier at the February Montgomery Convention, allowed for the election of a President and Vice-President in November 1861 to work alongside a Congress. The President and Vice-President were to be elected to hold office for six years but be entitled to only one term of office. In the meantime, however, provisional officers of state were required. There were a number of potential candidates for the position of President, although there was a reluctance to see one of the more radical pro-slavery figures elected as it was felt that this might act to dissuade states that had not as yet seceded, such as Virginia, from joining the Confederacy. There were also a number of candidates from Georgia; however, the inability of the representatives from that state to agree upon a single candidate meant that their position was weakened. In the event a compromise figure—Jefferson Davis from Mississippi—was elected unanimously on February 9, 1861, with Alexander Stevens from Georgia as his Vice-President. On February 16, Davis was introduced to the crowd at Montgomery by William L. Yancey, who said, "The man and the hour have met." This event was probably the first at which "Dixie" was played as the unofficial southern anthem. In addressing the crowd, Davis took a hard line: "The time for compromise has now passed. The South is determined to maintain her position, and make all who oppose her smell Southern powder and feel Southern steel." Two days later, in his inauguration speech, he was slightly more moderate. To complete his government, six additional cabinet positions were filled, with one representative coming from each of the secessionist states with the exception of Davis' own Mississippi.

Another view of Jefferson Davis' house.

Portrait of Confederate Postmaster-general John H. Regan.

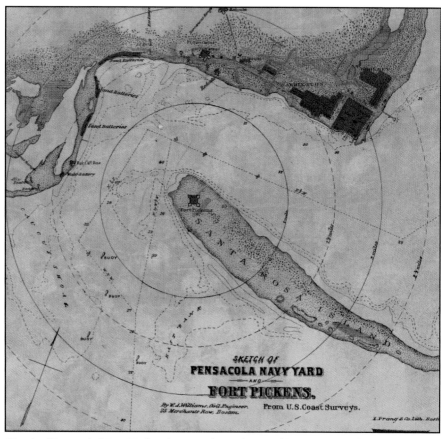

Sketch of Pensacola Navy Yard and Fort Pickens: they would remain in Federal hands throughout the war.

THE SOUTH ATTACKS FEBRUARY–APRIL 1861

James Buchanan remained President until March 4, 1861. In the period between the election and Lincoln assuming office, the position of the Union weakened as the secessionists successfully removed federal control from most of the military installations in the south until only two remained: Fort Pickens (off the Florida coast in the south, it would remain in Federal hands throughout the war) and Fort Sumter close to Charleston. It was to be the latter that witnessed the first shots of the war.

Fort Sumter, located on a granite island four miles from Charleston, was provided with 40-feet-high brick-built walls varying in thickness between 8 and 12 feet. It was designed to house some 146 large guns and be garrisoned by 650 men. Although it was designed primarily for protection from the sea, it was still capable of defense from landward attack. In December 1860, however, it was effectively unmanned, with the small federal garrison of some 80 men under the command of Major Robert Anderson, housed at the nearby Fort Moultrie.

Negotiations were taking place to secure the peaceful transfer of Fort Sumter to South Carolina. If events hand not overtaken Buchanan, it is probable that Sumter would have been ceded. However, on December 26 Anderson—a Kentuckian who had once owned slaves but who was vehemently in favor of the Union—moved his small force secretly into Fort Sumter, thereby causing Carolinian accusations of treachery. In early

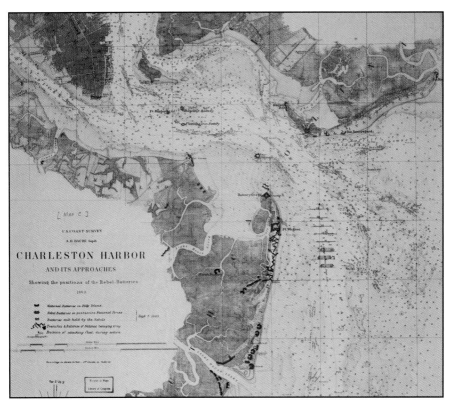

1863 map of Charleston Harbor showing Fort Sumter and the position of Union and Confederate forces on September 7.

1861, the federal General-in-Chief, Scott, sent 200 reinforcements on board the Star of the West but the vessel was fired on while approaching Charleston—arguably the first shots of the war—and retreated.

In Washington, with the arrival of Lincoln, the period of vacillation was over. Initially, his cabinet was in favor of further negotiations and his Secretary of State (Seward) actively pursued them, but Lincoln realized that northern public opinion would never agree to surrender the fort. Gradually, his cabinet came to the same conclusion. On April 4, aware that supplies in the fort were running out, Lincoln decided to send a relief ship carrying only provisions. He notified the Secessionists what he was doing, knowing full well to that effect that he was in a strong position: if the food got through, he would gain more time to negotiate; if the relief ship were attacked, then the Secessionists would be guilty of starting the conflict.

On April 9, in Montgomery, the Confederate government under Jefferson Davis took the fateful decision to authorize General Pierre G. T. Beauregard to launch the attack. On April 12 the first shots were fired; a fierce exchange of ordnance then ensued with Anderson's limited force firing back with determination. The odds, however, were stacked against him and, on April 13, he asked for terms for surrender which were agreed. On the following day, Federal troop were evacuated from Fort Sumter; the only casualties they had suffered were two fatalities caused by an explosion on the 14th while they fired a ceremonial salute to mark their departure.

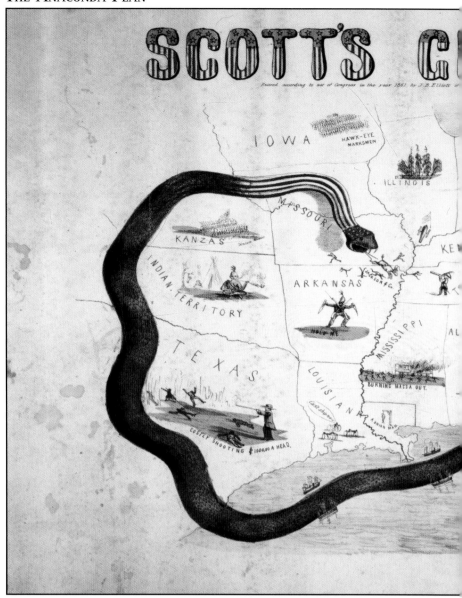

THE ANACONDA PLAN 1861

In early 1861, believing war to be inevitable, newly elected President Abraham Lincoln sought the advice of the veteran Commander-in-chief of the U.S. Army, Major General Winfield Scott. Scott's strategy was to force the breakaway states to re-enter the Union through a naval blockade of the Confederacy, taking control of the Mississippi River to split the Confederate states, and building up an army to protect Washington and tie down rebel forces in northern Virginia.

The intention was to exert increasing pressure on the Confederacy rather than to engage in large-scale offensive operations, which would drive the rebels further away from any reconciliation. However, popular opinion in the north regarded the plan as being too passive: it was nicknamed the "Anaconda Plan" because it proposed a slow constriction of the enemy rather than forcing a swift end to the war by marching directly on the Confederate capital, Richmond.

The immediate problem that Scott faced was to raise sufficient armies and naval vessels to put his plan into action. The U.S. Navy

LIEUTENANT-GENERAL SCOTT.

was inadequate to deal with the 3,500-mile-long Confederate coastline in early 1861 but a forceful program of construction, purchase, and conversion of merchant vessels saw the number of ships increase more than threefold by the end of the year. At the same time a volunteer army was rapidly being raised at Washington and by June Major General Irvin McDowell was in command of 30,000 troops at Arlington, outside Washington.

By late 1861 the U.S. Navy had amassed sufficient ships to enforce its blockade of the coastline. They were divided into four squadrons—the North and South Atlantic Blockading Squadrons, and the East and West Gulf Blockading Squadrons—and the economic strangulation of the Confederacy, which would grow throughout the war, was underway. However, political pressure, not least from Lincoln himself, meant that the Union strategy in their land campaign became more aggressive. Union armies simultaneously entered Virginia and Tennessee in July 1861 to outflank the Confederate forces and drive on toward Richmond. The advance was to be severely disrupted by the Union defeat at the Battle of Bull Run on July 21. By this time the Anaconda Plan had become overtaken by events and Scott retired on November 1, 1861.

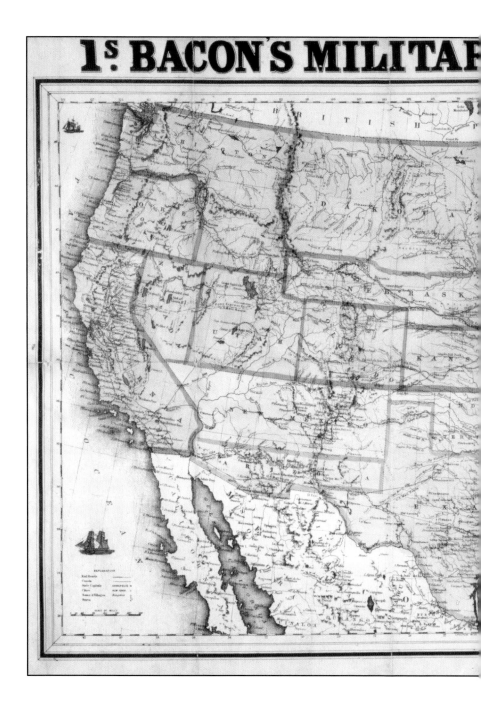

1ˢ BACON'S MILITAᴿ

THE CRITTENDEN RESOLUTION JANUARY 1861

Politicians in Kentucky had earned a reputation for trying to mediate between the anti- and pro-slavery states, as evinced by the efforts of Henry Clay in 1820, 1833, and 1850. By the final breakdown of relations, John Jordan Crittenden represented Kentucky in the Senate. He was one of 13 senators appointed to a special committee—there was also a parallel body established in the House of Representatives—which was set up to find a way to avoid the final break.

The Senate committee comprised five Republicans and eight Democrats, with Crittenden belonging to the latter camp. He proposed a compromise resolution amending the U.S. Constitution to guarantee

MAP OF AMERICA.1S

BACON'S
MILITARY MAP OF THE
UNITED STATES
Shewing the
FORTS & FORTIFICATIONS.

Published by BACON & C° 48 Paternoster Row.

LONDON 1862

EXPLANATION.

the rights of the slave owners. However, all five Republicans in the committee voted against the resolution, as did two of the Democrats, thus defeating the proposal by a margin of 7–6. Undaunted, Crittenden attempted to push the amendment through the Senate on January 16, 1861. He was defeated 25–23, with all 25 Republicans voting against the proposal. Although politically dead, the resolution kept bubbling under and even as late as May 1861 pro-Union citizens in Kentucky remained hopeful that the resolution could form the basis of another compromise. However, while Lincoln had hinted at the possibility of compromise when taking the oath of office in March 1861, no such amendment ever found its way onto the statute book.

Portrait of Abraham Lincoln

ABRAHAM LINCOLN CALLS FOR A MILITIA APRIL 15, 1861

On April 15, 1861, President Abraham Lincoln called on the governors of the Northern states to provide a militia of 75,000 men to serve for three months. This was how long he expected it would take to put down the insurrection, which he believed was "too powerful to be suppressed by the ordinary course of judicial proceedings."

The call for a militia led to pro-war rallies in many northern cities; in New York, for example, a city that had had leanings toward the south, 250,000 turned out for a rally, while even leading Democrats, such as Stephen Douglas, could come out in favor of action. He said, "There are only two sides to the question. Every man must be for the United States or against it. There can be no neutrals in this war, only patriots—or traitors."

Most states responded well to Lincoln's call. The governor of Pennsylvania offered 25 regiments, while that of Ohio proffered 22. Many states offered more regiments than they had been asked for; Indiana, for example, had been asked to supply six regiments, but the governor offered 12 while the governor of Ohio intimated that having filled the 13 regiments demanded he would be hard-pressed to stop recruiting at less than 20. In order to encourage men to join the new militia, the state governors offered bounties, or bribes, to the volunteers. Inevitably, the offer of money attracted the poor and the dispossessed to the newly created militia. There was also considerable support for it among the black population of the North; however, those attempting to join the army were turned away as the War Department announced that it had "no intention to call into service of the Government any colored soldiers." The army was, however, willing to recruit blacks for non-military duties such a camp attendants, cooks, and waiters.

Executive Mansion March 18th 1861.

To the Secretary of War:

Sir: You will favor me by issuing an order detailing Lieut. Ephraim E. Ellsworth, of the First Dragoons, for special duty as Adjutant and Inspector General of Militia for the United States, and in so far as existing laws will admit, charge him with the transaction, under your direction, of all business pertaining to the Militia, to be conducted as a separate bureau, of which Lieut. Ellsworth will be chief, with instructions to take measures for promoting a uniform system of organization, drill, equipment, &c. &c., of the U.S. militia, and to prepare a system of drill for light troops adapted for self-instruction, for distribution to the Militia of the several States. You will please assign him suitable office rooms, furniture &c. and provide him with a clerk and messenger, and furnish him such facilities in the way of printing, stationery, access to public records, &c. as he may desire for the successful prosecution of his duties; and also provide in such manner as may

be most convenient and proper, for a monthly payment to Lieut. Ellsworth, for this extra duty sufficient to make his pay equal that of a Major of Cavalry.

Yours obt Servt

Abraham Lincoln's letter to Simon Cameron, Secretary of War, on the creation of bureau of Militia, March 18, 1861.

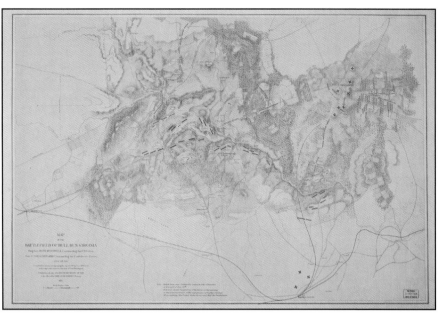

Map of the battlefield of Bull Run, Virginia, produced by the U.S. Army Corps of Engineers and published in 1877.

FIRST BATTLE OF BULL RUN JULY 21, 1861

When the Union and Confederacy slid into war in the early months of 1861, both sides started to raise volunteer armies, concentrated around northeast Virginia and Washington. By early summer, on the Union side Brigadier General Irvin McDowell and Major General Robert Patterson were in command of armies at Arlington, outside Washington, and Harpers Ferry further west. On the Confederate side Brigadier General Pierre G. T. Beauregard commanded a 22,000-strong army at Manassas Junction, and General Joseph E. Johnston was in command of 12,000 troops in the Shenandoah Valley.

Under political pressure to mount an immediate offensive to crush the rebellion despite the inexperience of his troops, McDowell devised a plan to take the strategically important railway junction at Manassas, keeping the two Confederate armies separate, which would leave the way open to advance towards Richmond, the Confederate capital. In July McDowell's 35,000-strong force began the advance towards Confederate northern Virginia. Although the Confederate forces barring the way were split into two, crucially they were linked by the Manassas Gap Railroad. Beauregard set up his forces on the south side of Bull Run Creek, about three miles north of Manassas Junction railway station. The original Union plan had entailed Johnston's Confederates in the Shenandoah Valley being pinned down by Major General Robert Patterson's army, but by the time McDowell neared Beauregard's positions Patterson had withdrawn his forces to Harpers Ferry.

The first skirmishes between McDowell's and Beauregard's forces took place along the creek on July 18, with the Union troops being forced back at Blackburn's Ford. The two sides then faced each other across the creek, both making plans to attack. Crucially, Beauregard had time

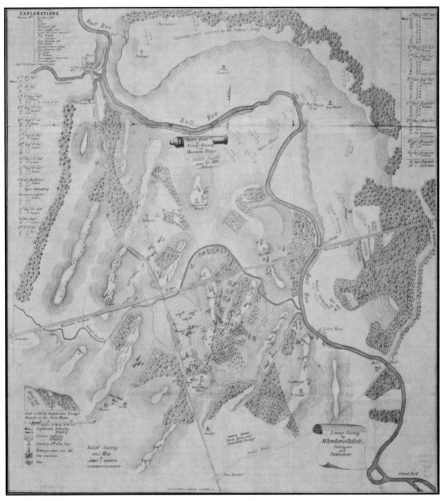

Another map of the battlefield of Bull Run/Manassas Junction.

to contact Johnson to request reinforcements be sent by rail, the first elements of these arriving on the 19th, swelling the Confederate army to over 30,000.

The main attack started on July 21. McDowell intended to launch two diversionary attacks, one at the stone bridge crossing Bull Run Creek and another further south at Blackburn's Ford and Mitchell's Ford, enabling his main force to outflank the Confederates on their left, to the north, at Sudley Springs. Union troop movement started at 02:00 and did not reach the creek until several hours later, at 05:00 when three brigades under Brigadier General Daniel Tyler reached the stone bridge. Meanwhile the planned main attack of two divisions under Brigadier Generals David Hunter and Samuel P. Heintzelman set off on the long, circuitous march towards Sudley Springs, the leading brigade only crossing the creek at the undefended ford at 09:00.

To stabilize his line, Beauregard was forced to call off his planned attack on the Union left from Blackburn Ford. Colonel Nathan G. "Shanks" Evans, who had managed to hold the bridge for the Confederates against Tyler, received a signal that he was about to be outflanked by Union troops approaching from Sudley Springs Ford. He

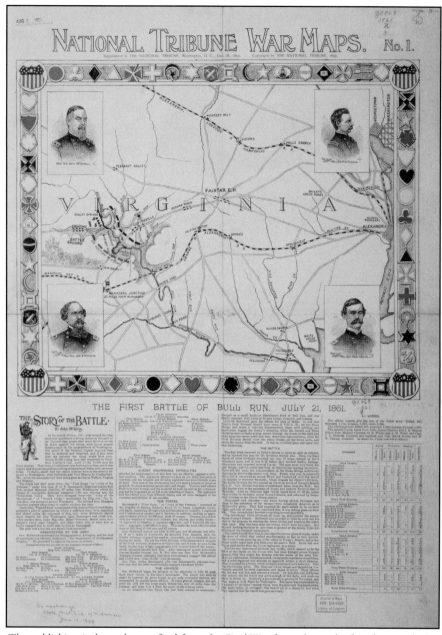

The publishing industry has profited from the Civil War from almost the first shot, producing books, magazine articles, and maps on the subject.

turned his men and, with the assistance of Brigadier Generals Barnard Bee's and Francis S. Bartow's brigades on high ground at Matthew's Hill, repelled Hunter's leading flanking assault from the north as it emerged from the woods onto open ground just after 10:00.

However, the Union troops kept the momentum of their attack going. Tyler and two brigades managed to cross the creek at a ford near the stone bridge. At the same time the next flanking column—led by Heintzelman—attacked the Confederate line in the northwest, driving it off Matthew's Hill, across the Warrenton Pike and Young's Branch of Bull Run Creek, back toward Henry House Hill. It was at this stage—at 11:15—that the two Confederate generals Beauregard and Johnston, who were with their forces in the vicinity of Blackburn's Ford, realized

Dedication of the battle monument at Bull Run, Va., June 10, 1865, as photographed by William Morris Smith.

the main battle was taking place to the north of their HQ and set off in the direction of the gunfire. They arrived at Henry House Hill in time to join the Confederate Brigadier General Thomas J. Jackson who had established his brigade in a defensive position on the hill earlier in the day, and were able to organize the retreating Confederate troops into a defensive line on the high ground.

The climax of the battle would take place at the top of Henry House Hill. The retreating Confederate forces had reached the hill in a disorganized rabble, and in a famous exchange Bee had told Jackson that they were unable to contain the Union troops' advance. In reply, Jackson suggested Bee rally his men around his Virginian brigade. Bee then pointed to Jackson, exhorting his men to rally round him—"There stands Jackson like a stone wall"—thus coining the subsequent nickname "Stonewall" Jackson by which the legendary Confederate general became known.

The Union troops attacked at 13:00, five brigades charging up the hill supported by artillery, but the Confederate line held firm despite the loss of Bee, killed in this first attack. Throughout the afternoon the Confederates repulsed a series of ferocious but uncoordinated attacks. For a while the battle hung in the balance, typified by the struggle over two Union artillery batteries, which had been ordered onto the hill by McDowell and which changed hands three times in fierce hand-to-hand fighting.

Matthews' or the Stone House at Bull Run, Va.

By 16:00 the Union troops were becoming increasingly exhausted and disorganized, many beginning to drop out of the battle, and the arrival of Confederate reinforcements allowed Beauregard to launch an attack on the Union left. The now-demoralized Union troops fled from the battlefield across Young's Branch toward the stone bridge. Shots were fired by a Confederate battery at the Union troops as they crossed Bull Run Creek, some swimming the river, but the Confederates were too exhausted themselves to pursue them through the countryside towards Washington and their defensive positions around Fairfax Courthouse.

Although the Battle of Bull Run (known to the Confederates as the Battle of Manassas) was to have no lasting strategic significance, and losses were low compared to later battles fought by much more experienced and battle-hardened troops, this was the first major battle of the war and the victory was a boost to Confederate confidence.

Cub Run, Va.: view with destroyed bridge.

PARTICIPATING UNITS:

Confederates: ....General Joseph E. Johnston, Army of the Shenandoah, 9,000 men; Brigadier General Pierre G. T. Beauregard, Army of the Potomac, 24,000 men, total 33,000

Union: ....Brigadier General Irvin McDowell, Army of Northeast Virginia, 35,000 men

THE BATTLE:

Duration of battle: ...10 hours; July 21, 1861

Location of battle: ....Bull Run Creek/Manassas Junction, Virginia

Outcome: ....Confederate victory

CASUALTY FIGURES:

Confederates: ....387+ killed, 1,582 wounded—estimated 2,000 casualties in total

Union: ....460 killed, 1,124 wounded, 1,312 missing—estimated 3,000 casualties in total

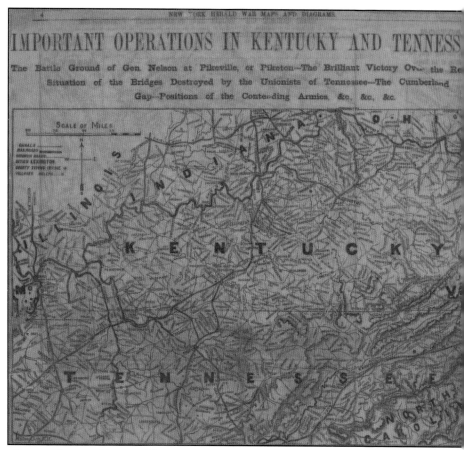

The seat of war in Missouri. The important points of the war, showing the positions of the rebels under Generals McCulloch and Price, and the advance of the Union troops under Generals Fremont, Hunter, Siegel [sic], Sturgis.

FRÉMONT'S PROCLAMATION AUGUST 30, 1861

John C. Frémont was an experienced soldier. Known as the "Pathfinder of the West," he had spent 11 years with the army's topographical department. He was, therefore, an obvious candidate when Lincoln sought to appoint a new commander of the army in Missouri in July 1861. However, once in command, Frémont proved inadequate, facing a Confederate force that adopted guerrilla tactics.

In order to improve his position against the Confederate guerrillas and to garner favor with Republicans, Frémont issued a proclamation on August 30, 1861, whereby he claimed to have taken over "the administrative power of the state." The proclamation declared martial law, announced the death penalty for those guerrillas caught behind Union lines, and confiscated the property of all Confederate activists in the state as well as freeing all their slaves.

In the short term his actions found favor with some Republicans, but Lincoln was vehemently opposed to the measure, fearing, for example, that summary execution of guerrillas would lead to retribution against Union soldiers caught by Confederate forces. He asked Frémont to modify his proclamation on the lines of the act passed by Congress on August 6, 1861, which only confiscated the property of those directly involved in the war effort. Frémont, however, was adamant, sending his daughter, Jessie, to convince Lincoln. This policy backfired as a result of

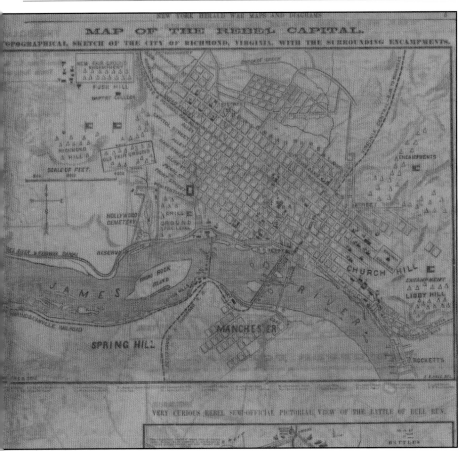

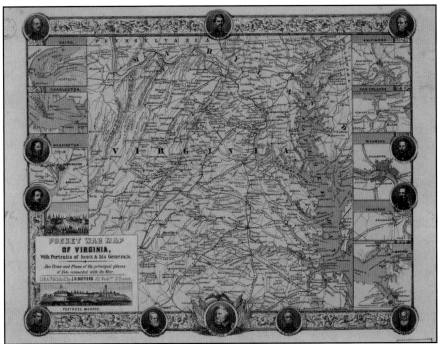

Pocket war map of Virginia, with portraits of Scott, Harney, McClellan, Sprague, Frémont, Butler, Banks, Dix, Lyon, McDowell, Mansfield, and Wool.

antipathy between Lincoln and Jessie Frémont, and as a result, Lincoln ordered Frémont to change the statute. Further military defeats, however, resulted in Frémont being relieved of his command and Lincoln took the step, personally, of revoking the proclamation.

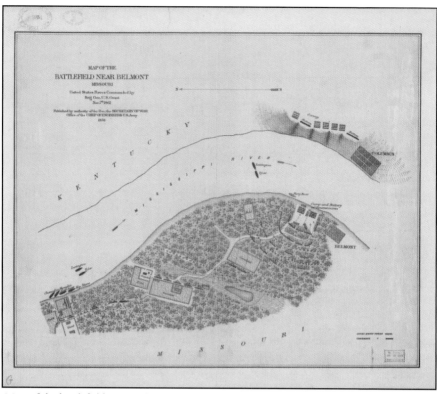

Map of the battlefield near Belmont, Missouri, United States forces commanded by Brig. Gen. U.S. Grant, November 7, 1861.

GRANT IN KENTUCKY AUTUMN 1861

The western theater of the Civil War was no less strategically important than the eastern. The border states of Kentucky, Missouri, and Tennessee would be crucial. Each sent men to fight on both sides and control of these states would open up the Union or Confederacy to the opposing side, particularly along the rivers. The Mississippi, Tennessee, and Cumberland rivers penetrated deep into Confederate territory and the Ohio opened the way to the Union states of Ohio, Indiana, and Illinois.

Kentucky originally declared itself neutral but on September 4, 1861, Confederate Major General Leonidas Polk led a small army of 12,000 men into southeastern Kentucky to seize the town of Columbus on the Mississippi River. The Union had also been building up its forces under Brigadier General Ulysses S. Grant in nearby Cairo, Illinois. He immediately retaliated by entering Kentucky with an army of 20,000 men from the Western Department and occupying Paducah on the Ohio River. Large armies from both sides then entered Kentucky and the Confederate General Albert S. Johnston, who had succeeded Polk as commander of Department Number Two, which covered several states in the west, set up a defensive line known as the "long Kentucky line." This ran across the south of Kentucky from Columbus, through Forts Henry and Donelson on the Tennessee and Cumberland Rivers respectively, east to Bowling Green, where his main force was located, and the Cumberland Gap.

Portrait of Ulysses S. Grant as a major general: Lincoln had promoted him from brigadier general in September 1862 after he had taken Fort Donelson.

The Union forces were split into two overall commands in the west. Major General Henry W. Halleck commanded the Department of Missouri centered on St Louis; Brigadier General Don Carlos Buell at Louisville was in command of the Department of the Ohio. Because of this split, the Union response was not coordinated. Buell moved slowly toward Bowling Green in the autumn of 1861, but Halleck dispatched Grant in a more aggressive sequence of probing attacks on the western end of the Confederate defensive line. He had at his disposal the gunboats of the Mississippi River Squadron, based at Cairo, led by Flag Officer Andrew H. Foote.

The Union gunboats engaged the Confederate shore batteries at Columbus on October 7. Then in early November 3,000 men moved down the Mississippi River on steamers protected by the gunboats Lexington and Tyler to raid Confederate positions at Belmont, Missouri, where a chain blocking the river had been set up. On November 7 Grant landed his forces and attacked the garrison at Belmont, driving off the defenders. Each side lost approximately 600 men in the first major battle of the western theater. Although Major General Leonidas Polk, in command of the main Confederate forces across the river at Columbus, sent 10,000 troops to cut Grant's men off from their transports, the Union troops managed to reach their boats and escape.

Thereafter, Grant realized that Columbus was too well defended for a direct attack and began to prepare for his next move, which would bypass the town by moving down the Tennessee and Cumberland rivers to attack Forts Henry and Donelson.

The Union's blockade of the South was increasingly effective. This photograph shows the Confederate blockade runner Robert E. Lee *at Norfolk, Va., after it had been taken. It was renamed the U.S.S.* Fort Donelson.

THE TRENT INCIDENT NOVEMBER 8, 1861

The southern states sent ministers James Murray Mason and John Slidell to persuade the major European powers of the era to intervene in the American Civil War on the part of the Confederacy. Britain, in particular, was not unsympathetic. By the 1860s, the massive growth of the cotton industry in Britain, fed by raw materials supplied from the slave states, was such that many thousands of jobs were reliant upon the secure supply of raw cotton. The Union blockade threatened this supply and, during the course of the war, economic stagnation severely affected the industry. In addition, while British politicians were opposed to the maintenance of slavery, if Britain had backed the Confederacy to achieve victory, it would undoubtedly have strengthened British influence in the New World.

The two officials slipped through the northern blockade but the Union naval commander in the region, Captain Charles Wilkes, became aware of their presence on Cuba where they had boarded the British mail-steamer Trent. Wilkes seized the Trent and forced the vessel into Boston harbor, where Mason and Slidell were incarcerated in Fort Warren.

Britain reacted with hostility, threatening war and reinforcing her forces in Canada. Ultimately, to prevent war, which neither Britain nor the Union wanted—Lincoln commented, "One war at a time." The two were released in December and allowed to complete their journey. In the end, however, the mission was to prove fruitless as neither Britain nor France intervened on behalf of the Confederate states.

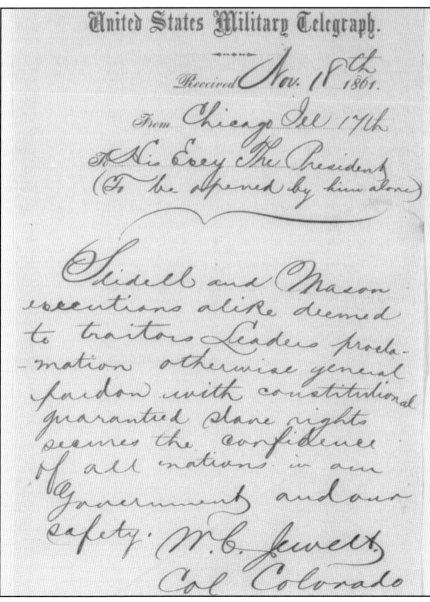

Telegram detailing the capture of Slidell and Mason

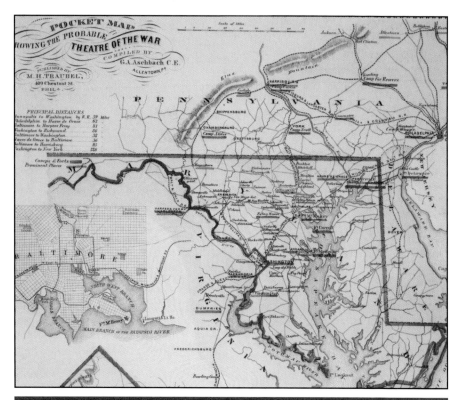

MCCLELLAN TAKES COMMAND NOVEMBER 1861

Born in 1826, George Brinton McClellan—nicknamed "Little Mac"—graduated from the U.S. Military Academy at West Point in 1846 and served with distinction during the Mexican War. A military engineer, he worked on a number of major projects including the survey for a Northern Pacific railway across the Cascade Range in 1853–54. In May 1861 he was made commander of the Department of the Ohio with the rank of major general in the regular army. In June and July 1861 he cleared the western part of Virginia. Following the Union defeat at the first Battle of Bull Run, he was given command of the troops around Washington. In November 1861 he was made Union general in chief, although his ability was temporarily impaired in December 1861 when he went down with typhoid. Unfortunately, during his time in Washington, he spent much of his energy conspiring against his fellow officers, earning himself another—and less complimentary—nickname: "The Young Napoleon."

He was summoned by Lincoln to train the new Army of the Potomac. While he was undoubtedly popular with his troops as he was unwilling to sacrifice lives needlessly and brought improved discipline to the army, he was perceived by Lincoln and public opinion as overly cautious, if not timid. It was McClellan that drew up the strategy that lay behind the Peninsular Campaign but, before his force reached the southern tip of Virginia, at Fort Monroe between the York and James rivers, Lincoln had reduced McClellan's position, removing him from the rank of general in chief. Lincoln had good reason to be concerned about McClellan's abilities as, during the Peninsular Campaign and the Seven Days' Battles, the general proved himself to be a poor judge of Confederate strength and ultimately missed the opportunity to capture Richmond.

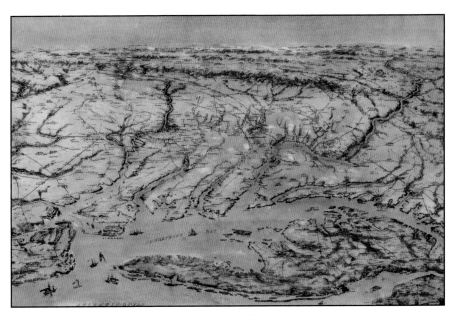

Left and Above: The seat of war in Virginia, Maryland, Delaware, and around the Potomac and Chesapeake Bay.

Portrait of Maj. Gen. George B. McClellan and his wife, Ellen Mary Marcy.

Probing attacks by the Union on the Confederates' long defensive line in southern Kentucky in autumn 1861 demonstrated the potential threat posed by the Union's superior naval power. The rivers, which ran deep into Confederate territory, were weak spots in the defensive line so Confederate General Albert S. Johnston, who had command of all Confederate forces from the Appalachian mountains to the Mississippi, ordered the construction of forts along the rivers. Chief of these were Fort Henry on the Tennessee River and Fort Donelson on the Cumberland.

In spite of the forts General Ulysses S. Grant planned to attack the Confederates down these rivers so that he could avoid the more heavily defended Confederate stronghold of Columbus on the Mississippi. On February 3, 1862, Grant embarked from Cairo with a force of 15,000 men carried on river transports and escorted down the Tennessee River by a fleet of shallow-draft ironclad gunboats, commanded by Flag Officer Andrew Foote. Fort Henry was only lightly defended and following a bombardment from Foote's gunboats on February 6, the Confederate commander, Brigadier General Lloyd Tilghman surrendered, without Grant's troops having to fire a shot. Tilghman ordered his infantry to retreat to the nearby Fort Donelson, 12 miles east and Grant's next objective.

Fort Donelson was in a stronger defensive position high above a bend of the Cumberland River, with two creeks to the landward side, and batteries comprising 12 heavy guns and eight additional field guns. The garrison initially numbered 6,000, under the command of Brigadier General Bushrod R. Johnson. To reinforce the defenders General Albert S. Johnston sent two divisions—one under Brigadier General John B. Floyd, who assumed command of the fort; the other commanded by Simon B. Buckner—from his main army at Bowling Green, and a further detachment under Brigadier General Gideon Pillow, bringing total Confederate numbers to around 21,000.

FORT HENRY

PARTICIPATING UNITS:

Confederates: ....Brigadier General Lloyd Tilghman, 3,000 men of Department # Two

Union: ....Brigadier General Ulysses S. Grant, 15,000 men of Department of the Missouri; Flag Officer Andrew H. Foote, seven gunboats from the Mississippi River Squadron

THE BATTLE:

Duration of battle: ....1.5 hours; February 6, 1862
Location of battle: .....Fort Henry, Tennessee
Outcome: ....Union victory

CASUALTY FIGURES:

Confederates: ....20 casualties; 80 surrendered
Union: ....40+ casualties

The winter weather slowed Grant's progress along the roads from Fort Henry but by February 12 his infantry and cavalry were in position to besiege Fort Donelson. Grant first attacked on the Confederate left on the 13th but was beaten back. The next day his force was reinforced by a division sent from Major General Don C. Buell's army near Bowling Green, under Brigadier General "Lew" Wallace, and the same day Grant launched a serious assault on the fort. At 15:00 Foote took six gunships, which had arrived the night before, to attack the fort from the river. However, the Confederates' batteries inflicted heavy damage to the fleet, seriously wounding Foote, and by the end of the day it became clear that the fort's defenses were too strong for a water-borne assault.

Fort Donelson's commanders decided they could not survive a siege and planned to break out through Grant's lines and escape to the south. In the morning of the 15th the Confederates attacked and broke through Grant's right wing, leaving the way open for the garrison's forces to escape towards Nashville. However, confusion and hesitation between the Confederate commanders led to their advance being halted and by the end of the day the Union, despite losing 2–3,000 men compared to Confederate losses of about 500, pushed the Confederates back to their original defenses. During the night the Confederate generals decided that they were unable to break out and had no option but to surrender the garrison. Floyd and Pillow escaped upriver with two Virginian regiments, Colonel Nathan B. Forrest took his Tennessee cavalry regiment along an unguarded route and on the morning of February 16 Buckner requested a cease-fire to discuss surrender terms. Grant famously replied, "No terms except an unconditional and immediate surrender can be accepted." Buckner was forced to order the remaining 13,000 men in the garrison to lay down their arms. The loss of Fort Donelson was a serious blow to the Confederates as it broke open Johnston's defensive line, forcing him to fall back through Tennessee.

FORT DONELSON

PARTICIPATING UNITS:

Confederates: ....Brigadier General John B. Floyd, 21,000 men of Department # Two

Union: ....Brigadier General Ulysses S. Grant, 15,000 men of Department of the Missouri; Brigadier General Lewis Wallace, 11,000 men of Army of West Tennessee; total 26,000 Flag Officer Andrew H. Foote, six gunboats from the Mississippi River Squadron

THE BATTLE:

Duration of battle:....4 days; February 13–16, 1862
Location of battle:.....Fort Donelson, Tennessee
Outcome:.................Union victory

CASUALTY FIGURES:

Confederates: ....2,000+ casualties including 500 killed; 13,000 captured
Union: ....Under 3,000 casualties

James River, Va. Deck and turret of U.S.S. Monitor.

BATTLE OF HAMPTON ROADS MARCH 8–9, 1862

At the start of the war the Confederates realized that they had to build up a navy to defend the vast coastline of their territory, as well as their inland waterways. Faced with the much larger U.S. Navy, the Confederate Secretary of the Navy, Stephen Russell Mallory, decided to put his faith in new technology, particularly the use of ironclad floating batteries.

The opportunity to build the first ironclad ship quickly presented itself when the Union abandoned its dockyard at Norfolk, Virginia, and failed to fully destroy one of the steam frigates there, the U.S.S. Merrimac. The Confederates managed to raise the hull and salvage the sunken engines, and built an ironclad superstructure upon her, rechristening her Virginia. She was armed with ten guns, both smooth-bored and rifled.

News that the Confederates were building an ironclad leaked out to the Union and, concerned at the vulnerability of their all-wooden-hulled fleet, the U.S. Secretary of the Navy Gideon Welles commissioned a radical armored ship from a Swedish designer, John Ericsson. The ship, U.S.S. Monitor, would be smaller than its Confederate rival, with only two guns mounted in a revolving turret. Its design was radical, however: its shallow draft meant it was more maneuverable, its lack of superstructure gave it a low profile in the water, and the guns were mounted in a fully revolving turret enabling them to be brought to bear rapidly in any direction.

Soon after C.S.S. Virginia was completed, she set sail from Norfolk on March 8, 1862, to attack Union shipping in Hampton Roads. Under the command of Flag Officer Franklin Buchanan she attacked and sank U.S.S. Cumberland then set fire to U.S.S. Congress later that day before returning to harbor.

The Union feared that the way was open for Virginia to steam up the Potomac and bombard Washington. Fortunately for their cause, Monitor had been recently completed the previous month and was dispatched under the command of J. P. Bankhead to the assistance of the remaining U.S. Navy warship at Hampton Roads, the U.S.S. Minnesota. Arriving that night, Monitor was in position to take on the Virginia when she sallied forth again the next morning. Firing at close-quarters, the two ironclads battered each other for four hours without causing serious damage. However, despite the Monitor having to use smaller charges than usual for fear of her guns exploding in the turret, the Virginia suffered more in the exchange, and Buchanan was wounded. Her smokestack was riddled with shot which meant that her underpowered engines struggled still further in a vain attempt to ram the more agile Monitor and she withdrew from the battle.

Despite the inconclusive nature of the battle, this first encounter between two ironclads marked a new era in naval warfare and both sides went on to produce more armored ships following the prototypes they had established. The two ships themselves never met again—the Confederates destroyed Virginia later in the war to prevent her falling into Union hands and the unseaworthy Monitor sank while under tow past Cape Hatteras.

PARTICIPATING UNITS:
Confederates: .............C.S.S. Virginia (Flag Officer Franklin Buchanan)
Union: .....................U.S.S. Monitor (Commander J. P. Bankhead)

THE BATTLE:
Duration of battle: ....4 hours; March 9, 1862
Location of battle: .....Hampton Roads, Virginia
Outcome: ....Stalemate; Virginia withdrew but neither ship seriously damaged

CASUALTY FIGURES:
Wounded only

Portrait of Maj. Gen. John A. McClernand.

BATTLE OF SHILOH APRIL 6-7, 1862

After Fort Donelson fell Major General Grant's Union forces from the Department of the Missouri pushed deep into Tennessee along the Tennessee River. General Albert S. Johnston was forced to pull his Confederate defensive line back to the vital railroad junction at Corinth, Mississippi, allowing Major General Don C. Buell to take Nashville, Tennessee in late February 1862 with his Army of the Ohio. By the end of March Grant's army had reached Pittsburgh Landing on the Tennessee River, where nearly 40,000 men pitched camp at a site called Shiloh, after a nearby church. The plan of Major General Henry W. Halleck, recently appointed overall commander of Department of the Mississippi, was for Buell's force to join that of Grant at Pittsburgh Landing, whereupon he would lead the combined armies in an overwhelming attack on Johnston at Corinth. On March 15 Buell started to dispatch his 37,000-strong army on its 120-mile march toward Pittsburgh Landing, but it would take some three weeks to reach Grant.

Meanwhile Johnston was preparing his own plan of attack. Realizing the vulnerability of his position at Corinth once the Union had combined forces, and that while Grant was isolated he had temporary parity in numbers with just over 40,000 men under his command, he decided to act quickly. He gathered his forces at Corinth under the recently created Army of the Mississippi—I Corps under Major General Leonidas Polk comprised four brigades; II Corps under Major General Braxton Bragg comprised six brigades; and III Corps under Major General William J. Hardee comprised three brigades. In addition, Brigadier General John C. Breckinridge was moving up from the south with the Reserve Corps of three brigades and Lieutenant General Pierre G. T. Beauregard arrived from the Army of the Potomac with a small number of troops to act as Johnston's second-in-command.

Mortar destroyed in fighting at Fort Pulaski.

On April 3 the Confederate army set off from Corinth. The sheer number of soldiers on the roads and heavy rain slowed the advance and it was not until April 5, a day later than planned, that Johnston's men were in position to attack. Unbelievably, Grant was unaware of the imminent presence of the Confederate army within two or three miles of his camp, and when Johnston launched his attack at dawn on April 6 the Union troops were caught completely by surprise, Grant himself having spent the night away from the camp at Savannah. In Grant's absence Brigadier General William T. Sherman was in command of the sprawling Union camp without any defensive lines, and his division was plunged into chaos by the first wave of the Confederate attack. Because of the fierce fighting, many of the men on the Union side fled and that story was repeated in the first few hours of fighting with the next two Union divisions commanded by Brigadier Benjamin M. Prentiss and Major General John A. McClernand, which were driven back towards the Tennessee River.

However, the formation adopted by Johnston also created confusion in the Confederate ranks. The three corps of Hardee, Bragg, and Polk were arranged over a three-mile front, one behind the other, and once the fighting began it became increasingly difficult to exercise effective command in the melee. Crucially for the Union, about 4,300 of Prentiss' men with reinforcements from Brigadier General William H. L. Wallace's division managed to rally in a heavily wooded area in the center of the Union line at 09:30. In the course of the day they held off 12 Confederate attacks from 11:00, in which the fighting was so fierce that the area subsequently became known as the "Hornet's Nest." During one of the attacks, at 14:00, Johnston himself rode up to the front line to urge the men on. A stray bullet struck him in the leg but, unaware he had been wounded, he continued to press the men to attack until he fell

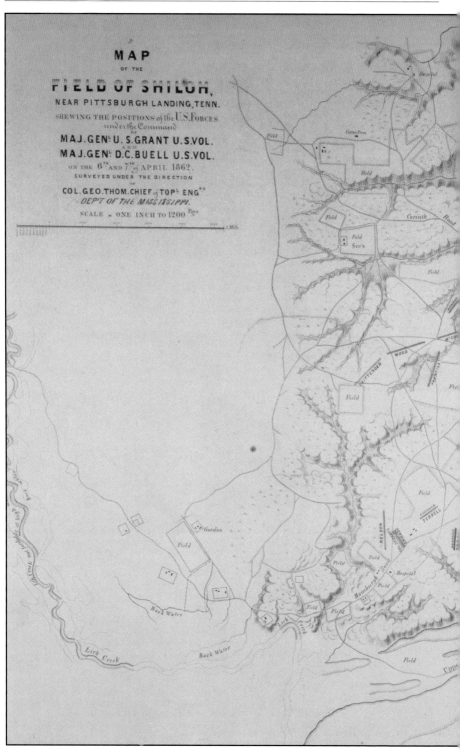

Map showing the battle of Shiloh.

unconscious due to loss of blood and died at about 14:30. Beauregard, in the rear, assumed command but the event increased the Confederate confusion. Although the Union troops in the "Hornet's Nest" were finally outflanked and Prentiss surrendered the remnants of his men late in the day, at approximately 17:30, they had slowed the Confederate advance and bought precious time.

The noise of gunfire that morning had brought Grant hurrying south and he arrived at the battlefield at midday. Despite the overwhelming

nature of the initial Confederate attack, the plan to push hardest on
the Union right, nearest the Tennessee River, thereby driving Grant's
forces away from the river, had stalled. Nevertheless, apart from in the
"Hornet's Nest," the Union troops were gradually being forced on both
flanks against the river. On the Union right, first Sherman's command
had collapsed by about 10:30, then Major General John McClernand's
division was forced to retreat; on their left Brigadier General Stephen
A. Hurlbut's division was being squeezed towards the river. For a while
there was confusion in the Confederates' ranks once the "Hornet's Nest"
surrendered; many thought the battle was over and started to plunder the
Union camps. However, Generals Bragg, Polk, and Breckinridge quickly

Sketch of the battle of Shiloh—Union in blue; Confederates in red.

met at 18:00 and decided to seize the day, issuing the order to "Sweep everything forward and drive the enemy into the river." The position looked desperate for Grant. All day he had waited for reinforcements from Buell's army and from Major General "Lew" Wallace's division, which had been guarding the Union rear at Crump's Landing.

Grant's desperate efforts to shore up the Union line received a boost when the first of Buell's men arrived on the battlefield in the late afternoon followed by Wallace's men who belatedly arrived at 19:15. By this stage the Confederate attack had run out of steam and Beauregard, realizing his men were exhausted, called a halt to the fighting at nightfall, intending to renew the assault on the Union lines the next morning.

Overnight, Grant received a huge boost to his forces as the bulk of Buell's Army of the Ohio arrived, giving him another 15–20,000 men in the field. Deciding to press home his advantage in numbers, Grant launched a counterattack on the Confederates at 07:30 on the second day of the battle, attacking across the whole front with his rejuvenated forces. The fighting matched the first day in its intensity but slowly the Confederates were driven back until, by the end of the morning, the Union had regained all of the ground lost in the previous day. By 14:30 Beauregard could see that his outnumbered men were spent and ordered a general retreat back to Corinth. Grant felt his troops were not strong enough to pursue them and by midafternoon the battle was over.

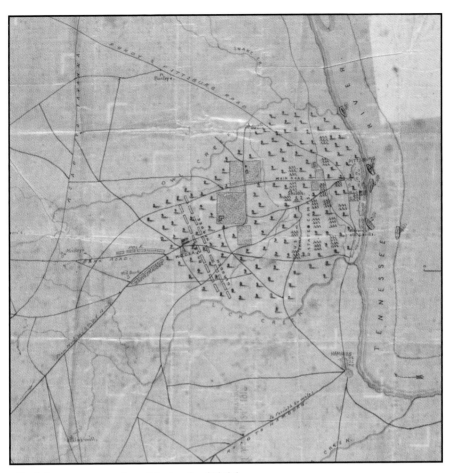

Confederate representation of the battle of Shiloh.

Shiloh (known by the Confederates as Pittsburg Landing) had been the bloodiest battle of the war up to date, with both sides suffering heavy losses. Johnston's gamble to forestall the Union advance into Tennessee had so nearly succeeded, but as the Confederates had failed to destroy Grant's army and the Union troops still held the field, the Union could claim the battle as a victory and they were still in a position to renew their drive towards Memphis and Corinth.

PARTICIPATING UNITS:

Confederates: ....Army of the Mississippi, General Albert S. Johnston, 44,000 men

Union: ....Army of Tennessee, Major General Ulysses S. Grant, 40,000 men; (Second day) Army of the Ohio, Major General Don C. Buell, 15,000 men; total; 55,000

THE BATTLE:

Duration of battle:....Two days; April 6–7, 1862

Location of battle:.....Camp Shiloh (Pittsburg Landing), Tennessee

Outcome: ....Union victory

CASUALTY FIGURES:

Confederates: ....Approx 10,700 casualties—1,723 killed, 8,012 wounded, and 959 missing

Union: ....Approx 13,000 casualties—1,754 killed, 8,408 wounded, and 2,885 captured

The band of 107th U.S. Colored Infantry at Fort Corcoran, Arlington, Va.

HUNTER BEGINS ENLISTING BLACK SOLDIERS MAY 1862

David Hunter was born in Washington on July 21, 1802, and graduated from the Military Academy at West point 20 years later. Prior to the Civil War he had seen active service in both the Seminole (1838–42) and Mexican (1846–48) wars. An opponent of slavery, he had corresponded with Lincoln and was invited to Washington in January 1861. At the outbreak of war, he joined the Union army and became colonel of the 3rd U.S. Cavalry. Recovering from wounds received at Bull Run in July 1861, he replaced John C. Frémont as commander of the Western Division. In March 1862 he was appointed Commander of the Department of the South.

After a successful campaign at Fort Pulaski, he began enlisting black soldiers—although these were more conscripted than volunteers—from the freed slaves of the occupied districts of South Carolina, and organized them into the 1st South Carolina Volunteer (African Descent) Regiment during May 1862. He was, however, initially ordered to disband the regiment with many people—Lincoln, for example—disapproving of his action. However, the 37th Congress, concluded its second session enacting two laws on July 17, 1862, covering the creation of a militia and also empowered the President to enroll "persons of African descent" for "any war service for which they may be found competent." One Senator commented, "The time has arrived ... when military authorities should be compelled to use all the physical force of this country to put down the rebellion." Thus, after the event, Hunter's action was approved and from July 1862 onward increasing numbers of those of African ancestry joined in the struggle. Hunter himself created two further black regiments in 1863.

Maj. Gen. David Hunter took Fort Pulaski, Ga., in April 1862. A fierce 30-hour bombardment "softened up" the defenders. This interior view of the front parapet shows the damage done. The loss of the fort effectively closed Savannah to blockade runners.

"Stonewall" Jackson's Confederate camp with soldiers gathered in prayer, many leaning on their swords.

Jackson's Valley Campaign March–May 1862

The Shenandoah Valley in Virginia was vital to the Confederates' cause. Running from Harpers Ferry in the north to Staunton in the south, it was the chief food-producing region in the state and its defense was assigned in November 1861 to a 16,000-strong army led by Confederate Major General Thomas J. ("Stonewall") Jackson. The Union was aware of the strategic significance of the valley, and in February 1862 Major General Nathaniel P. Banks led an army of 38,000 men into the northern entrance of the valley. Jackson's smaller force retreated in the face of this advance, which reached Winchester, the first major town in the valley, before Banks had to return two divisions to assist in the defense of Washington.

In an attempt to prevent Banks' men reinforcing McClellan's army at Washington, Jackson launched an attack with 4,000 infantry against one of Banks' divisions, 9,000-strong, at Kernstown, near Winchester on March 23. The attack was driven off easily and after two hours Jackson was forced to withdraw his forces, having suffered 718 casualties compared to Union losses of 590. Despite the Union victory, President Lincoln regarded Jackson as a threat and ordered Banks to remain near Harpers Ferry with 9,000 men. He also decided to retain a large force to the north of the valley to keep Jackson away from Washington as well as ordering Major General Irwin McDowell to move his 40,000-strong corps of the Army of the Potomac from its base at Fredericksburg west to cut off Jackson at the south of the valley. Jackson reacted swiftly. He marched his men rapidly south to forestall a third Union force of 15,000 approaching the valley from West Virginia, under the command of Major General John C. Frémont. Making use of the railroad to Staunton, Jackson adopted a defensive position on high ground nearby and defeated Frémont's detachment at the Battle of McDowell on May 8.

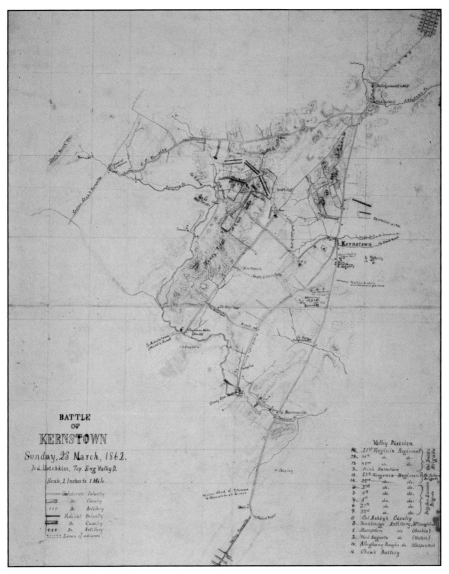

Battle of Kernstown, Sunday, March 23, 1862.

Jackson then moved his forces with mesmerizing speed north along the valley toward Banks, earning his soldiers the nickname of "foot cavalry," taking a small Union garrison at Front Royal on May 23 before catching up with Banks' main force on May 25. Jackson attacked Banks' defenses in the ensuing battle of Winchester and the Union line broke, the men being pursued in disorder to the Potomac River.

However, Jackson was again threatened with being cut off by the convergence of Frémont's and McDowell's forces and turned south for another rapid march. Before the two Union armies could close he attacked and defeated Frémont's force at the Battle of Cross Keys on June 8 before turning the next day on a division of McDowell's corps led by Brigadier General James Shields at Port Republic. Jackson was again victorious and Lincoln ordered a halt to Frémont's and McDowell's advance: the Valley Campaign was over. In three months Jackson had won five out of six battles, kept the valley free for the Confederates and tied down up to 60,000 Union men in a fruitless campaign.

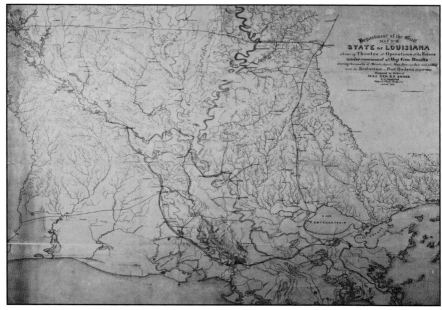

Map of Louisiana showing New Orleans; the map was produced in January 1863 for Maj. Gen. Nathaniel Banks.

Farragut takes New Orleans April 1862

David Glasgow Farragut (1801–70), although born in Tennessee and married to a Virginian, was a staunch supporter of the Union. First serving at sea at the age of nine, he was a veteran of both the War of 1812 and that against Mexico. In February 1862 he took command of a fleet that comprised eight steam sloops—the sand bars at the mouth of the Mississippi precluded the use of frigates—one sailing sloop, 14 gunboats, and 15 mortar schooners as well as transports for the 15,000 soldiers under Benjamin Butler. By early April, this fleet was approaching New Orleans, but was faced initially by the forts that guarded the river to the south. Initially Farragut's tactics were to pound these forts at the rate of 300 shells per day from his mortar schooners, but this had little effect and so, early in the morning of April 24, he sent two gunboats to breach the boom that stretched across the river. With the action now in full swing, Farragut sent his force through the breached boom, engaging the shore-based forts in an exchange of gunfire that, ultimately, was to cost the lives of 37 Union sailors. The Confederates responded as best they could, attempting to ram Farragut's ships, gaining one success when the Varuna was sunk. In addition, the Confederates also launched fireships in an attempt to destroy the Union fleet. Unfortunately, from the Confederate standpoint, the ironclads under construction were ill-prepared for action. Having successfully negotiated this first part of the city's defenses, Farragut destroyed the batteries immediately to the south of the city the following day. If he had expected an immediate surrender, he was denied and so he ordered his troops to take the city on April 29; two days later, soldiers under Butler entered the city.

Rear Adm. David G. Farragut, promoted to vice admiral from December 3, 1864.

Bird's eye view of the seat of war around Richmond, showing the battle of the Chickahominy River, June 29, 1862.

THE PENINSULAR CAMPAIGN MARCH–MAY 1862

In early 1862 the Union General-in-Chief, McClellan, formulated a plan that he believed would result in the rapid capture of Richmond. Taking advantage of the Union's control of the seaways, McClellan proposed shipping an army to Fort Monroe, at the tip of the peninsula formed by the James and York rivers, and then march the 70 miles to Richmond. This route involved only two minor river crossings; Lincoln, however, was not wholly convinced, preferring an overland route. Despite this, Lincoln gave the project the go-ahead and the Union's Quartermaster General, Montgomery Meigs, put together the invasion force. This was to comprise, ultimately, some 400 vessels to transport 100,000 men, 300 canons, 25,000 animals, and the provisions that the army would require.

To McClellan the beauty of the proposal was the supposed ease of resupply via sea. However, in the period prior to the assault, Lincoln acted to reduce McClellan's power. On March 8, Lincoln created four new corps commanders without consulting McClellan and, three days later, reduced him from general in chief to the position of commander of the Army of the Potomac alone. There were sound strategic reasons for such an action since McClellan's field command precluded him from taking a strong strategic overview, but it was symptomatic of Lincoln's doubts over his commander. In addition, a new military department, for West Virginia, was created under the command of General Frémont. Another factor that weakened McClellan's position was the perceived threat from the Confederate forces under Jackson in the Shenandoah Valley; although defeated by Nathaniel Banks at Kernstown on March 22, Jackson was considered to have greater resources than he possessed in reality. This resulted in Lincoln refusing to sanction the transfer of part of Banks' force to McClellan. The consequence was that, ultimately,

Portrait of Brig. Gen. Montgomery C. Meigs, Quartermaster-General of the Federal Army. He was promoted to major general from July 5, 1864.

McClellan had an army of only 100,000 rather than the 150,000 he had hoped for.

McClellan's force landed at Fort Monroe on March 17 and by early April was facing Confederate forces at Yorktown. McClellan's lack of will to succeed was demonstrated at Yorktown where, facing only 13,000 Confederate troops under John Magruder, he failed to press home an assault. Ultimately, Magruder was to withdraw himself during the night of May 3/4 and, on May 5, James Longstreet undertook a strong rearguard action at Williamsburg to ensure the orderly retreat of Confederate forces and delay yet further the Union advance.

Having abandoned the naval yard at Norfolk, including the destruction of all military equipment there (including the C.S.S. Virginia), the Confederates ceded control of the rivers to the Union and, in order to capitalize on this, a Union flotilla, including the Monitor, sailed upstream intending to shell the city. However, strong Confederate gunfire from the batteries at Drewry's Bluff on May 15 prevented the Union fleet from reaching its target.

By this stage, McClellan was only six miles from Richmond. However, his army was situated on both sides of the Chickahominy River, a watercourse bloated by unseasonably heavy rain during April and May and crossed by only temporary bridges, and this gave the Confederate defense the opportunity to attack one wing of the Union army. Following heavy rain on May 30, most of the temporary bridges were washed away and, on the following day, Johnston launched his counterattack. However, the Confederate force was confused, with Longstreet, for example, taking the wrong road; the result was a delayed assault. Although Union forces were driven back, reinforcements led

1 Old Point Comfort
2 Fortress Monroe
3 Water Battery
4 Hampton Roads
5 Rip Raps
6 Chesapeake Bay
7 Sewall's Point
8 Craney Island
9 Eliza
10 Norf
11 Ports
12 Dism

Fortress Monroe, Va., and its vicinity.

by Edwin Sumner, which had managed to cross the river, prevented a Confederate victory at Seven Pines (or Fair Oaks as it became known to the Union). One consequence of the battle was that Johnston was injured, to be replaced as commander by Robert E. Lee. One of Lee's first actions was to send 1,200 men under Jeb Stuart to reconnoiter the Union lines; a round trip of some 100 miles. This allowed Stuart to provide his commander with the detailed information to launch the next phase in the war in the peninsula, a phase that would become known as the Seven Days' Battles.

Right: Group of the Irish Brigade at Harrison's Landing, Va.

at court of the United States, for the southern district of New York.   R. Hinshelwood.

iver	13 Atlantic Ocean	17 Newport News
	14 Cape Hatteras, N.C.	18 Hampton
	15 Nansemond River	19 Mill Creek
amp.	16 James River	20 Land approach to Fortress.

Fair Oaks, Va. Prof. Thaddeus S. Lowe observing the battle from his balloon "Intrepid."

Battle of Seven Pines (Fair Oaks) May 31, 1862

As we have seen, following the Union defeat at Bull Run in July 1861, Union Major General George B. McClellan had been under pressure to devise a new plan of attack against the Confederate capital, Richmond. To avoid Confederate General Joseph E. Johnston's large army at Manassas he would move his army by water to the Virginia coastline, from where he could march directly on Richmond. In March 1862 he landed his 105,000 men of the Army of the Potomac at Fort Monroe on the Yorktown peninsula, to embark on the Peninsular Campaign.

By late May McClellan had advanced to within ten miles of Richmond but Johnston was facing him with an army of 60,000 men, having retreated slowly up the peninsula. The Confederates were established behind the Chickahominy River, which bisected the peninsula. McClellan made the mistake of splitting his advancing army in two, the largest part of his force moved north of the river but he placed two corps (40,000 men under Major General Samuel P. Heintzelman and Major General Erasmus D. Keyes) south of the river.

Heavy rain in May made the river impassable along much of its course, particularly isolating Keyes, and Johnston saw his chance to strike a damaging blow against McClellan's divided forces. He planned to hold the bulk of McClellan's army north of the Chickahominy with the divisions of Major General Ambrose P. Hill and Major General John B. Magruder, while the divisions of Major General James Longstreet reinforced by Brigadier General William H. C. Whiting, Major General Daniel H. Hill, and Major General Benjamin Huger would attack Keyes simultaneously.

Battery M., 2nd U.S. Artillery, commanded by Capt. Henry Benson, seen near Fair Oaks.

The Confederates attacked on the morning of May 31 but confusion over orders caused chaos on the narrow roads when Longstreet led his men across Whiting's and Huger's advance. In the north, A. P. Hill and Magruder were successfully holding Brigadier General Fitz J. Porter and Brigadier General William B. Franklin, but D. H. Hill waited in vain for the main left wing attack led by Longstreet. By 13:00 Hill could wait no longer and launched his attack on Keyes' men at Fair Oaks. He managed to force the Union troops back to their second line at Seven Pines, held by the majority of Keyes' corps, but there the weakened Confederate attack stalled, as the Union forces were bolstered by reinforcements from Brigadier General Edwin V. Sumner's corps from north of the river.

At nightfall the Confederates withdrew toward Richmond, General Johnston having been seriously wounded in the fighting at Fair Oaks. He would be replaced in command by Robert E. Lee. Despite having been victorious at the Battle of Fair Oaks, McClellan had been taken aback by the ferocity of the fighting and for the rest of the campaign would proceed cautiously.

PARTICIPATING UNITS:

Confederates: ....General Joseph E. Johnston, Army of Northern Virginia, 60,000

Union: ....Major General George B. McClellan, Army of the Potomac, 100,000

THE BATTLE:

Duration of battle:....One day; May 31, 1862

Location of battle:.....Fair Oaks station/Seven Pines, Virginia

Outcome: ....Union victory

CASUALTY FIGURES:

Confederates: 6,000   *Union:*..............5,000

The Army of the Potomac's encampment at Cumberland Landing, Va., on the Pamunky River.

THE SEVEN DAYS' BATTLES JUNE–JULY 1862

Fought between June 25 and July 1, 1862, the Seven Days' Battles represented a critical phase of the efforts by the Union Army of the Potomac, under McClellan, to press on and capture Richmond in Virginia. The various engagements all took place to the east of the city and were ultimately to result in a Confederate strategic victory with McClellan's army in retreat, but one that was to cost the Confederate army dear in terms of casualties.

The overall Confederate commander, Robert E. Lee, designed a plan to weaken the Union position by secretly moving Jackson's Shenandoah Valley army to oppose them. In his planning and as the events progressed, he had one great advantage: McClellan constantly overestimated, both in his own mind and in his reports to his superiors, the size of the Confederate force. This failing meant that he failed to capitalize on the points within the series of battles that could have been used to the advantage of the Union army by a more aggressive general. The total force available to the opposing sides were of the order of 87,000 for the Confederates and 105,000 for the Union. Rather than exploiting this advantage, McClellan, who had learned of the approach of Jackson's force on June 24, sought rather to explain to his masters in Washington why conditions were not appropriate for an assault and, by doing so, he handed the strategic advantage to Lee.

The first engagement of this phase occurred on June 25 when Union troops reconnoitering the area around Seven Pines came into contact with the Confederate force. In a skirmish at Oak Grove, about 500 men from both sides were either killed or injured.

Supply vessels at anchor at White House Landing, Va.

The following day witnessed the Battle at Mechanicsville; this was to prove, according to McClellan, a "complete victory," but he failed to take advantage of his victory as, being aware of Jackson's somewhat tardy approach, he told Porter to withdraw four miles during the night of June 26/27 to a stronger defensive position at Gaines' Mill, behind Boatswain's Swamp. In addition, McClellan also withdrew slightly, to a base by the James River, an action which emphasized that he had, to all intents, abandoned his planned assault on Richmond itself.

Savage Station, Va. Field hospital after the battle of June 27

20-pdr. Parrott rifled guns of the 1st New York Battery near Richmond, Va.

The Battle of Gaines' Mill occurred on June 27; this engagement also witnessed failures within the Confederate command structure with the result that, while it was ultimately to prove a Confederate victory, the losses incurred significantly weakened Lee's forces. As McClellan again withdrew, Lee hoped to strike at the retreating army's flank, but he was thwarted by geography, weakness of commanders, and a continuing failure on the part of Jackson to energize his section of Lee's army.

The failure of Jackson's force throughout this phase of the war is surprising; it may well be that his army was exhausted after its rapid move to the region, but later historians have seen Jackson's failure during the Seven Days' Battles as a major factor behind the Confederates' inability to take advantage of their strategic position.

The next engagement occurred on June 29 at Savage's Station, when Magruder attacked a Union rearguard; the Union forces easily saw off the Confederates. Again the Confederate position was undermined by the actions of Jackson, who was delayed in his approach by a decision to construct a temporary bridge rather than simply to ford the river. The scene was now set for the final battle of this phase: Malvern Hill on July 1. This engagement again proved costly for the Confederates who were ultimately to be defeated, although, once again, McClellan failed to take advantage. The disproportionate role of Hill and Jackson during the battles is best exemplified by casualty statistics: whilst Hill's force represented about 15% of the total manpower available to Lee, it suffered 21% of the casualties. Conversely, Jackson's army presented 21% of the total but suffered only 14% in terms of casualties.

Lt. Robert Clarke, Capt. John C. Tidball, Lt. William N. Dennison, and Capt. Alexander C.M. Pennington pose for the camera near Fair Oaks, Va.

PARTICIPATING UNITS:

Confederates: ....Robert E. Lee, Army of Northern Virginia, 87,000

Union: ....Major General George B. McCLellan, Army of the Potomac, 105,000

THE BATTLE:

Duration of battle:....Seven days; June 25–July 1, 1862

Location of battle:.....Around Richmond, Virginia

Outcome: ....Union victory

CASUALTY FIGURES:

Confederates: 20,000

Union: 16,000

The Peninsula, Va. The staff of Gen. Fitz-John Porter; Lts. William G. Jones and George A. Custer reclining.

BATTLES OF MECHANICSVILLE AND GAINES' MILL JUNE 26 & 27 1862

The Battle of Mechanicsville—also known as Beaver Dam Creek or Ellerson's Mill—was the second of the Seven Days' Battles. A total of 15,631 Union troops under Brigadier General John Porter faced 16,356 Confederate soldiers under Robert E. Lee.

The battle was initiated when Lee launched an offensive against McClellan's right flank north of the Chickahominy River. The Confederate position was weakened by the tardiness of Jackson's arrival, but the battle was started by A. P. Hill throwing his division, supported by one of D. H. Hill's brigades, against Porter's V Corps. There was no good reason for Jackson's delay, other than possible tiredness from his quick march to the theater, and the fact that the Confederates were unable to commit the overwhelming force that Lee had planned for—a 60,000 army would have been available if Jackson had been present— meant that the Union army was able to drive back Hill's forces with heavy casualties. Despite this victory, McClellan aware that Jackson was quickly approaching the vicinity, ordered Porter to retreat to a stronger defensive position, setting the scene for the third of the Seven Days' Battles—Gaines' Mill.

The attack at Gaines' Mill occurred on June 27 and was marked by poor coordination between Lee and his divisional commanders. The plan called for A. P. Hill to attack Porter's center, whilst Longstreet was to make a feint towards Porter's left flank and Jackson was to attack the Union right with four divisions. If Porter shifted his line to defend himself on the right, then all 55,000 of the Confederate force would be sent against his 35,000. Again, however, Jackson was slow to respond with the result that Hill again found himself attacking the Union lines without support, taking thereby heavy casualties. As the day wore on,

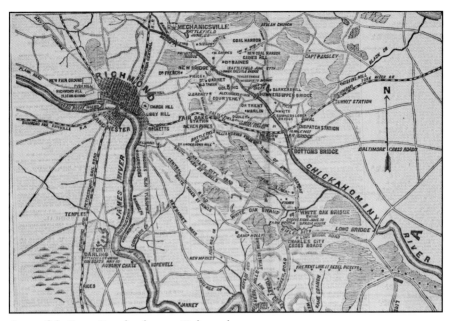

Scene of the Seven Days battles near Richmond.

however, Longstreet's army became increasingly prominent, launching a number of disjointed attacks and Jackson's also became engaged, thereby relieving much of the pressure from Hill's beleaguered forces. Towards dusk, the Confederates achieved a breakthrough in the center, led by the Texan John Bull Hood. With his line breached, Porter's defensive position collapsed and V Corps started to retreat. That the battle did not turn into a rout is explained by the fact that McClellan had sent reinforcements to assist Porter and these fresh troops helped to ensure an ordered retreat. This defeat at Gaines' Mill was one of the factors that persuaded McClellan to abandon his advance on Richmond and thus the victory at Gaines' Mill saved Richmond for the Confederacy at this time.

The ruins of Gaines' Mill.

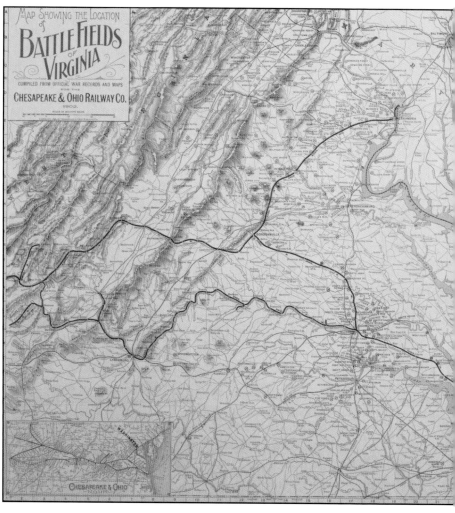

Ellerson's mill, Mechanicsville, Va.

Chickahominy River, Va. Bridge on Mechanicsville road

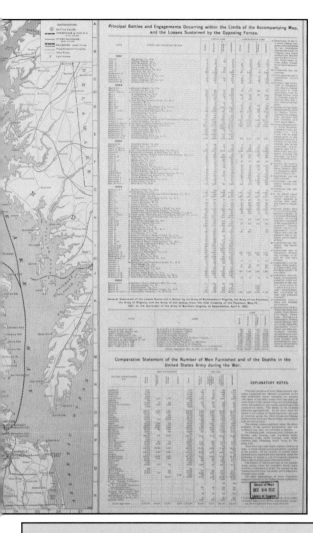

Battlefields of Virginia

GAINES' MILL

PARTICIPATING UNITS:
Confederates: ....Robert E. Lee, 57,518
Union: ....Brigadier General John Porter, 34,214

THE BATTLE:
Duration of battle:....June 27, 1862
Location of battle:.....Hanover County, Virginia
Outcome: ....Union victory

CASUALTY FIGURES:
Confederates: ....9,000 killed or injured
Union: ....2,800 taken prisoner; 4,000 killed or injured

MECHANICSVILLE

PARTICIPATING UNITS:
Confederates: ....Robert E. Lee, 16,356
Union: ....Brigadier General John Porter, 15,631

THE BATTLE:
Duration of battle:....June 26, 1862
Location of battle:.....Mechanicsville, Virginia
Outcome: ....Union victory

CASUALTY FIGURES:
Confederates: 20,000
Union: 16,000

Confederate bronze mountain howitzers.

BATTLE OF MALVERN HILL JULY 1, 1862

Following the engagement on June 30 at Glendale, the final battle in the Seven Days' Battles occurred at Malvern Hill on July 1, 1862. The Union Army of the Potomac under McClellan had retreated to a strong defensive position on the hill, 150ft in height and flanked by ravines one mile apart, located three miles from Glendale near to the James River. The hill could only be taken by a frontal assault and to defend it McClellan possessed four divisions and 100 guns with a further four divisions and 150 guns in reserve. The opposing Confederate force, under Robert E. Lee, had been strengthened through the capture of 30,000 small arms and 50 cannon from the retreating Union forces. Lee was also confident that the Union forces, being on the retreat, would be demoralized; in this he was partly right—McClellan was certainly feeling the strain—but when it came to a fight the Union army proved more resolute than its commander.

One of Lee's officers, James Longstreet (known affectionately by Lee as "My Old Warhorse"), had identified two positions from which he believed that the Confederate artillery could weaken the Union positions before frontal assault. On the morning of July 1, 1862, the Confederate bombardment began; however, it was ineffective and the Union gunners quickly responded with more success. Despite the failure of the artillery bombardment, Lee still launched his frontal assault with disastrous consequences. Thousands of Confederate soldiers were killed and injured by the artillery—some 5,500 in total during the battle—in an engagement which saw, uniquely for the American Civil War, more casualties caused by artillery than rifle fire. One of Lee's commanders, David Harvey Hill, commented that the battle "was not war—it was murder."

The best-known and most effective field piece of the war was the M1857 light 12-pdr., also called the Napoleon. Smoothbored, made from bronze, it could fire accurately to 1,600 yards.

Although the Union forces now had the upper hand, McClellan refused to advance to attack Lee's army and, following a truce, both sides buried their dead and withdrew to lick their wounds.

The Model 1841 6-pdr. smoothbore field gun, used extensively by the Confederates, was thought to be obsolescent by the Union.

PARTICIPATING UNITS:
Confederates: ....Robert E. Lee, Army of Northern Virginia
Union: ....Major General George B. McCLellan, Army of the Potomac

THE BATTLE:
Duration of battle: ....July 1, 1862
Location of battle: .....Henrico County, Virginia
Outcome: ....Union victory

CASUALTY FIGURES:
Confederates: 5,500
Union: 3,000

Battlefield of Cedar Mountain, Va., viewed from the west.

BATTLE OF CEDAR MOUNTAIN AUGUST 9, 1862

The Battle of Cedar Mountain was a pivotal moment in the battle for Virginia, marking as it did a shift in the military focus from the Peninsula to the Rappahannock River between Richmond and Washington. The battle took place 20 miles to the north of Gordonsville, itself northwest of Richmond, Virginia, and was the result of an action led by Thomas J. "Stonewall" Jackson (1824–63) against two of John Pope's advanced divisions under the command of Nathaniel P. Banks. Although Jackson's forces outnumbered his own by a ratio of two to one, Banks, in the belief that his own force was shortly to be reinforced, launched his own attack on August 9, 1862.

Initially, Jackson mishandled the battle with the result that the Union forces gradually gained the upper hand, forcing part of the Confederate force back. After this initial phase of the battle, Jackson sought to rally his troops and part of his army, under A. P. Hill, severely punished the Union force in a strong counterattack. Following this setback, Banks retreated, having lost about a third of his forces but it was at this point that his reinforcements arrived. Jackson, appreciating the fact that the balance of the battle had turned against him, was forced to retreat.

Federal battery fording a tributary of the Rappahannock on the day of the battle of Cedar Mountain.

Troops building bridges across the north fork of the Rappahannock.

PARTICIPATING UNITS:
Confederates: ....Major General Nathaniel P. Banks Corps, 8,030
Union: ....Major General Thomas J. Jackson Corps, 16,868

THE BATTLE:
Duration of battle:....August 9, 1862
Location of battle:.....Culpeper County, Virginia
Outcome: ....Union victory

CASUALTY FIGURES:
Confederates: 1,307
Union: 1,400

Culpeper Court House, with a group of Confederates captured at Cedar Mountain on balcony.

Union graves on the battlefield, Cedar Mountain, Va.

A Confederate field hospital, Cedar Mountain, Va.

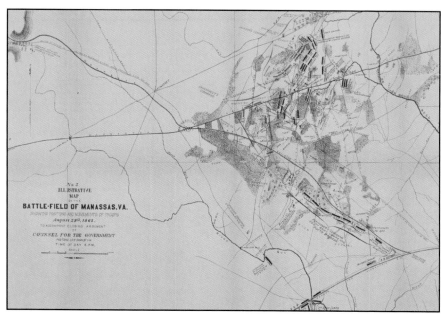

Illustrative map of the battlefield of Manassas, Va., showing positions and movement of troops, August 29, 1862

SECOND BATTLE OF BULL RUN (OR MANASSAS) AUGUST 29–31, 1862

As Major General George B. McClellan's Peninsular Campaign became bogged down outside Richmond by furious Confederate attacks, President Lincoln came to the conclusion that the Union needed to stretch the Confederates further if they were to achieve victory. He brought east one of his successful commanders from the western theater, Major General John Pope, and on June 26 he was given command of the 45,000-strong Army of Virginia, which had been newly formed from disparate units in northern Virginia and Maryland. His task was to advance on Richmond overland through Virginia, to open a second front on the Confederate capital.

It took time for Pope to organize his new forces, but by the start of July he was ready to advance into Confederate Virginia. By this time it was clear to Lee that McClellan had run out of steam on the peninsula so he dispatched Major General Thomas J. Jackson with 12,000 men, soon reinforced to 17,000, to counter the threat. Jackson's corps clashed with an advance corps of Pope's army led by Major General Nathaniel P. Banks at Cedar Mountain on August 9. Although Jackson emerged victorious, Pope was now alerted to the size of the force facing him and pulled his forces back north behind the Rappahannock River, Jackson withdrawing south of the Rapidan River. There Pope intended to wait for reinforcements as Lincoln, deciding the Peninsular Campaign had reached a dead end, ordered McClellan to withdraw his troops and transport them by ship north to join Pope.

Lee, realizing that McClellan was abandoning the peninsula, decided he needed to attack Pope before the two Union armies could combine. On August 13 he sent ten of his brigades, under the command of Major General James Longstreet, to join Jackson in the reorganized Army of

Bull Run, Va. New bridge built by McDowell's engineers.

Northern Virginia. The combined force then pushed north, crossing the Rapidan River again on August 20. Lee's plan was for Jackson's corps to outflank Pope, cutting off his supply lines, at which point the following Longstreet could join him in battle to defeat Pope. On August 25 Jackson set off with three divisions on a circular march round Pope's western flank. They reached Salem at the end of the first day and Bristoe Station the next day, having covered over 50 miles. There they cut the Union railroad, where Jackson left one of his divisions under the command of Major General Richard S. Ewell, before taking his other two divisions to ransack their supply depot three miles away at Manassas Junction. He then drew up his forces on a nearby low hill, along the line of an unfinished railroad, to wait for Pope.

On hearing the news of the attack on his supply lines, Pope marched north. He had received the first of his reinforcements from McClellan's command and now had 62,000 men at his disposal and expected Jackson to retreat in the face of his superior numbers. Brushing aside Ewell's division at Bristoe Station, he realized Jackson's whole corps was in his sights and ordered his commanders to concentrate their attack on Manassas. Pope's forces, however, were scattered in the area and on August 28 Jackson attacked a division of Brigadier General Irvin McDowell's corps as it was marching along the Warrenton Turnpike below his hidden position in the trees. Although he forced the Union troops to retreat from the field in the ensuing fierce fight, known as the Battle of Groveton, he had revealed his position to Pope.

Pope, however, still believed Jackson was on the retreat, and decided to split his forces to envelop the Confederates. He ordered McDowell's and Major General Fitz J. Porter's corps to occupy Gainesville, to the west of Jackson, to block Jackson's line of retreat and prevent the

Manassas Junction, Va. Soldiers beside damaged rolling stock of the Orange & Alexandria Railroad.

Confederates from getting any reinforcements through to him. The rest of the Army of Virginia would assault Jackson directly at Manassas. However, the plan received a massive blow when, unknown to Pope, Porter's corps was held up by Jackson's skirmishers at Dawkin's Creek while Longstreet was already marching his divisions through Gainesville to join Jackson.

On August 29 Pope drew up his forces on the site of the first battle at Manassas the previous year and at 13:00 launched a frontal assault on Jackson's dug-in troops. His attack was conducted piecemeal, however, units advancing in turn, which nullified the advantage in numbers held by the Union troops and Jackson's men were able to hold onto their positions. Concentrating on frontal assault Pope was unaware that Longstreet's corps of 25–30,000 men had reached the battlefield and were taking up position on the Confederates' right. When he finally ordered a flanking attack on Jackson, on the Confederates' right, Porter's men ran into Longstreet's lines and were repulsed, with Confederate artillery exacting a heavy toll. Porter was ordered to attack again but refused. He would be later court-martialed for his conduct in the battle.

Pope resumed his attacks on Jackson's line the next day, August 30, and this time Porter was to rejoin the attack but was repeatedly beaten back. Longstreet waited until the Union troops had completely exhausted themselves, and then at 16:00, when Jackson's troops were running out of ammunition, Longstreet's concealed artillery launched a devastating barrage at the Union line. His entire corps then charged the Union left which collapsed. Jackson's men joined the attack and drove the Union troops back to Henry House Hill, scene of some of the fiercest fighting in the first battle at Manassas/Bull Run. There the Union troops managed to regroup and make a stand, halting the Confederate advance. For the

Portrait of Brig. Gen. John Pope, who was promoted major general after March 21, 1862.

remainder of that day and the next they managed an orderly fighting retreat, managing to get across Bull Run Creek and reach Centerville by September 1.

Pope returned to Washington and was shortly afterward replaced in command by McClellan. Lee, meanwhile, despite the heavy losses sustained by the Confederates in the battle, was determined to retain the initiative and within days was invading Union territory in Maryland.

PARTICIPATING UNITS:
Confederates: .... General Robert E. Lee, Army of Northern Virginia, 55,000
Union: .... Major General John Pope, Army of Virginia, 62,000

THE BATTLE:
Duration of battle: .... Three days; August 29–31, 1862
Location of battle: ..... Manassas Junction, Virginia
Outcome: .... Confederate victory

CASUALTY FIGURES
Confederates: 9,000
Union: 16,000

A cavalry orderly at Antietam, Md.

BATTLE OF ANTIETAM SEPTEMBER 17, 1862

Immediately following his victory in the Second Battle of Bull Run and his earlier success in removing the threat to Richmond by driving the Union troops off the Yorktown peninsula, the way was open for General Robert E. Lee to enter Union territory. On September 4, 1862, he moved north from Manassas and crossed the Potomac River into Maryland with his 55,000-strong Army of Northern Virginia.

Opposing him was Major General George B. McClellan, who had been reinstated as overall commander of Union forces in the Washington and Virginia area after Pope's defeat at the Second Battle of Bull Run. Under his command was the newly formed Army of Potomac of 84,000 men, which incorporated the remains of Pope's Army of Virginia. In spite of his numerical disadvantage, Lee believed that McClellan's characteristic caution would allow him to seize the initiative with his invasion and on September 6 the Confederates occupied Frederick.

In fact, McClellan organized his men quickly and on September 7 they left Washington. During McClellan's subsequent slow approach, on September 9 Lee decided to split his army into several wings to take nearby Harpers Ferry, securing a vital supply line and also a possible line of retreat. Major General Thomas J. Jackson took three divisions on a roundabout march to Harpers Ferry, while another two divisions led by Major General Lafayette McLaws and Brigadier General John G. Walker completed the encirclement of the town but the Union garrison did not surrender until September 15. There Jackson left a division under Major General Ambrose P. Hill to secure the garrison and set off with his remaining divisions to rejoin Lee's main force.

In the meantime, Lee had temporarily dispatched Major General

The battlefield of Antietam on the day of the battle—September 17.

James Longstreet's two divisions north before moving his remaining divisions to South Mountain, west of Franklin, where he intended to take advantage of the terrain in the forthcoming battle with McClellan. McClellan was moving faster than Lee anticipated, however, spurred on by a stroke of good fortune: a copy of Lee's orders to his commanders detailing the planned movements to take Harpers Ferry fell into McClellan's hands when he entered Frederick on August 13. The next day Major General William B. Franklin on the Union left wing moved to intercept the Confederate supply lines to Harpers Ferry at Crampton's Gap, and on the right wing Major General Ambrose B. Burnside headed towards South Mountain. Neither attack was successful: Franklin, despite initial success, was deterred when he encountered a large Confederate battle line; at South Mountain the Confederates, although outnumbered, managed to hold off the Union forces and Lee was able to regroup his forces at the nearby town of Sharpsburg.

By this stage Lee realized that McClellan had intelligence of his battle plan and was moving fast, so he abandoned his intended offensive. Instead he concentrated his forces defensively along Antietam Creek, two miles west of Sharpsburg, awaiting the arrival of Jackson's divisions. He was in a precarious position: hemmed in by the Potomac River to his rear, even with the addition of Jackson's men he would have only 40,000 and had little time to prepare any entrenched defenses, whereas McClellan would be able to bring 75,000 men to the battlefield. Jackson arrived at Sharpsburg on the afternoon of the 16th; later in the day, the first Union units arrived on the high ground above Antietam Creek.

By nightfall both sides had drawn up their forces in their battle lines. Lee arranged his thin defensive line to cover the likely points of attack, running from Longstreet's divisions on his right, defending a bridge

Portrait of Maj. Gen. William B. Franklin, who commanded the right wing of the Federal Army

crossing the creek, and in the center in a sunken road, to Jackson's divisions on his left in woods and fields. McClellan's plan was to attack Lee's left with Major General Ambrose E. Burnside's divisions and right with Major General Joseph Hooker's divisions, hoping that Lee would weaken his center to reinforce his flanks, then administer the coup de grace with a massive attack in the center.

At dawn the next day, September 17, Hooker led I Corps in attack through cornfields on Jackson's corps to the north. In the fierce fighting the Confederate divisions of Brigadier Generals Alexander R. Lawton in the cornfield and David R. Jones in West Woods were decimated. However, at 17:00 Confederate Brigadier General John B. Hood, also positioned in the woods, counterattacked and the Union advance stalled.

The next Union wave followed at 07:30 when Major General Joseph K. F. Mansfield's XII Corps attacked West Woods through the cornfield.

Blacksmith shoeing horses at headquarters of the Army of the Potomac.

Mansfield was killed and Hooker wounded in the attack, but although the Confederates fought valiantly, they were gradually driven back out of the woods towards Dunker Church. At this stage the next Union attack was launched on the Confederate left at Dunker Church: in midmorning, by Major General Edwin V. Sumner's II Corps. Two of Sumner's divisions pushed on toward Major General Daniel H. Hill's men, hidden in the sunken road. From this natural defensive line the Confederates poured volleys of devastating fire into the advancing Union lines, earning the road the nickname "Bloody Lane," but despite cutting down the front lines of the advancing troops, the weight of the Union troops' advance enabled them to take the lane, albeit with heavy casualties—nearly half their losses for the whole battle. However, McClellan elected not to throw his reserve V Corps under Brigadier General Fitz J. Porter into the fray and by about 13:00 the fighting on the northern flank died down. The Confederates in the cornfield and West Woods pulled back and McClellan and Sumner agreed that their troops had fought themselves to a standstill and abandoned any further attacks by the Union right wing for the rest of the day.

The center of gravity of the battle then shifted south. Longstreet's corps had become severely depleted in the morning as reinforcements were called north and little more than two Georgia regiments under Brigadier General Robert A. Toombs remained to hold the crossings along Antietam Creek on the Confederates' right flank. However, it was not until 10:00 that McClellan gave Burnside, on the Union left, the order to advance. He had made the mistake of not reconnoitering the creek, which was easily fordable, and aimed his attack across a single well-defended bridge, which became known as "Burnside's Bridge." He finally succeeded in getting his corps across at 13:00, but delayed his attack on Longstreet's forces until 15:00. Although he drove the Confederates back

Harpers Ferry. View of town; railroad bridge in ruins. The battle of Antietam turned after Hill's march from here.

to the outskirts of Sharpsburg it was in vain. The battle was turned when A. P. Hill's division arrived after a 17-mile forced march from Harpers Ferry and drove Burnside back to Antietam Creek.

The two exhausted armies stopped fighting at nightfall, but remained in their positions. Lee, although still heavily outnumbered and in a precarious position, refused to retreat from the battlefield. The next day, however, the ever-cautious McClellan made no move to attack and Lee withdrew his men back across the Potomac.

It had been the single bloodiest day of the Civil War. The Union suffered 12,400 casualties, the Confederates 10–14,000. Although Antietam (called the Battle of Sharpsburg by the Confederates) dashed Confederate hopes of winning international recognition through bringing the war to Union territory, and was regarded by Lincoln and McClellan as a victory, Lee had managed to avoid annihilation and would pose a threat to Union forces for several years.

Bodies of Confederate dead gathered for burial after the battle.

President Lincoln and Gen. George B. McClellan in the general's tent, October 3, 1862.

PARTICIPATING UNITS:

Confederates: ....General Robert E. Lee, Army of Northern Virginia, 41,000
Union: ....Major General George B. McClellan, Army of the Potomac, 87,000

THE BATTLE:

Duration of battle:....One day; September 17, 1862
Location of battle:.....Sharpsburg/Antietam Creek, Maryland
Outcome: ....Union victory

CASUALTY FIGURES:

Confederates: ....10-14,000 casualties:1,546 dead, 7,750 wounded, 1,000+ missing
Union: ....12,400 casualties; 2,108 killed, 9,500 wounded, hundreds missing

An illustration President Lincoln writing the Emancipation Proclamation.

EMANCIPATION PROCLAMATION SEPTEMBER 22, 1862

At the start of the war, the aims of the Union were straightforward: to reunite the country. However, as the war progressed, these aims, particularly in the mind of Abraham Lincoln, were extended to include the broader concepts of democracy, freedom, and equality. One event emphasized this transition: the Emancipation Declaration of January 1, 1863.

The process that led to the declaration was not straightforward. It was a process that Lincoln had been contemplating for some time when he issued the preliminary declaration on September 22, 1862. There were a number of factors that moved him in this direction, most notably a belief that it was a justifiable aim of the war to remove its causes. But there were other factors. These included a need to bolster northern spirits at a time when the war was going against them; a belief that by announcing emancipation there would be widespread desertions from the plantations in the south thereby weakening the Confederate war effort; and also a hope that by making emancipation an overt war aim the Union would gain more support overseas, in particular from Britain. The ability to recruit blacks into the army would also assist the north's own manpower problem. Despite the obvious benefits, Lincoln had to tread carefully as it was not easy under the U.S. constitution for a president to take sweeping action against property (the fact that slaves were regarded as property had earlier assisted the north in refusing to return escaped slaves when so asked, claiming them as "contraband" legitimately seized during hostilities).

The idea of a declaration was first raised in Lincoln's cabinet in July 1862 and it was agreed by the cabinet the following month; however, it was also agreed that it could not be announced formally until the Union

Lincoln is seen writing, his foot on the U.S. Constitution. Ghouls and demons surround him on the furniture, the inkpot. Two paintings of saints of war are hung on the wall.

had achieved some military victory—an event which Lee's defeat at Antietam offered. The preliminary proclamation was couched carefully in order to avoid any legal complications—for example, it was stated that slaves would not be freed if their masters made peace by January 1863—and more detailed proposals were made on December 1, 1862. Although there was some opposition from within border states, the policy was endorsed by the House of Representatives and signed by Lincoln on January 1, 1863.

Following news of its adoption, there was widespread celebration and, in the south, it had the desired effect: large numbers of slaves deserted their plantations, more to aid escaping Union Prisoners of War and other actions that fundamentally weakened the Confederate war effort.

Portrait of Maj. Gen. Henry W. Halleck.

Battle of Corinth October 3–4, 1862

Following the Confederates' defeat at the Battle of Shiloh in April 1862 Confederate General Pierre G. T. Beauregard retreated with his forces to Corinth, before being forced to evacuate the town on May 29 in the face of the advancing Union forces under Major General Henry W. Halleck. Shortly afterward Beauregard was relieved of his command, replaced by General Braxton Bragg. In June Bragg moved the bulk of his army out of his HQ in Tupelo in preparation for an invasion of Kentucky and Tennessee but left behind Major General Earl Van Dorn to hold the Mississippi River with 15,000 men and Major General Sterling Price, also with 15,000 men, in Tennessee to keep watch on the Union forces in the area. West of the Tennessee River, the Union troops were now under the overall command of Major General Ulysses S. Grant. Grant had 46,000 men garrisoned at the major towns, including Corinth, Memphis, Jackson, Brownsville, and Columbus.

On August 11 Bragg ordered Van Dorn to move north and join Price in an attempt to isolate and attack Grant's widely dispersed forces. Grant, receiving intelligence of this Confederate move, dispatched Major General William S. Rosecrans' 10,000-strong Army of the Mississippi to try to intercept Price before he could join Van Dorn. Price was attacked by Rosecrans at Iuka, 20 miles east of Corinth, on September 19 but escaped the attempted encirclement, and on the 28th joined up with Van Dorn, who took command of the Confederate force of 22,000 men.

Van Dorn decided to attack Corinth, preceded by a feint to the north, believing it to be the gateway to Tennessee. Rosecrans was not deceived by Van Dorn's initial move north and pulled his troops, now numbering 23,000 with reinforcements from the Army of the Tennessee, within the extensive defenses around Corinth.

Portrait of Maj. Gen. William S. Rosecrans, who held Corinth against Van Dorn.

At 10:00 on October 3 Van Dorn reached the outer defensive line west of Corinth and attacked, Price breaking through the Union line and pushing them back to the inner defenses. When the fighting died down in the evening, Van Dorn was confident that he could take the town the next day. That night Rosecrans regrouped his men and as Van Dorn renewed his attack at 09:00 the next morning, Union artillery tore great holes in the advancing Confederate lines. The Confederates managed to reach Battery Powell and Battery Robinett, the scene of desperate hand-to-hand fighting, but by early afternoon it was apparent that the Confederates would be unable to take the town. At 14:00 Van Dorn ordered his troops to retreat, the next day withdrawing to Ripley despite some skirmishing. It had been the bloodiest battle of the war in Mississippi and marked the end of Confederate ambitions in northern Mississippi.

PARTICIPATING UNITS:

Confederates: ....Major General Earl Van Dorn, Army of West Tennessee, 22,000

Union: ....Major General William S. Rosecrans, Army of the Mississippi and reinforcements from the Army of the Tennessee 23,000

THE BATTLE:

Duration of battle:....Two days; October 3–4, 1862

Location of battle:.....Corinth, Mississippi

Outcome: ....Union victory

CASUALTY FIGURES:

Confederates: 4,838

Union: 2,359

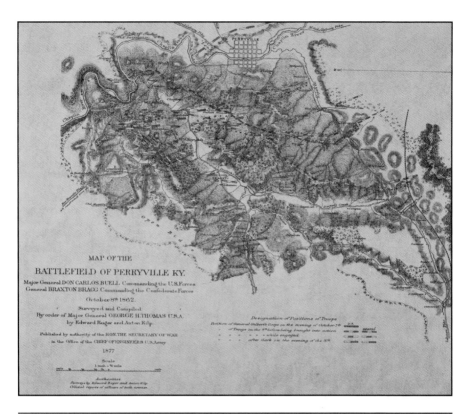

With both armies desperately seeking water towards the end of the campaign in Kentucky, a small force of some 16,000 men under the Confederate commander Leonidas Polk took up a defensive position on the Chaplin River at Perryville, Kentucky. On October 7, 1862, a single Union corps, commanded by Philip Sheridan, attempted to dislodge the Confederate force in order to gain access to the precious water. However, this initial assault proved unsuccessful and Sheridan was forced to withdraw. Early the following day, October 8, Sheridan again attacked, this time with more success and forced Polk's small force to retreat. Following this success, the rest of Don Carlos Buell's Union army joined up at Perryville; however, the Confederate commander, Braxton Bragg, unaware that the Union forces had been strengthened, ordered a reluctant Polk to launch a counterattack.

Two of Polk's three divisions attacked the Union left, where a new division broke under the Confederate assault forcing the entire Union left to retreat. In the center, however, Sheridan had more success, but as a result of topographical and atmospheric conditions—known as "acoustic shadow"—the Union commander, Buell, on the Union right, was unaware of the battle until a courier reported to him. By this stage it was too late for him to launch the remaining Union forces against the smaller Confederate army. The following morning, October 9, Buell ordered a new assault, but discovered that the Confederate force, aware of the imbalance, had withdrawn during the night. In terms of casualties, the Confederate force fared better but in terms of the strategic balance neither side gained: the Confederate force had failed to capitalize on its invasion of Kentucky and the Union had not achieved a stunning victory.

Portrait of Lt. Gen. Leonidas Polk.

PARTICIPATING UNITS:
Confederates: ....General Braxton Bragg, Army of the Mississippi
Union: ....Major General Don Carlos Buell, Army of the Ohio

THE BATTLE:
Duration of battle:....Two days; October 7–8, 1862
Location of battle:.....Boyle County, Kentucky
Outcome: ....Union victory

CASUALTY FIGURES:
Confederates: 3,400
Union: 4,200

Houses in Fredericksburg damaged by the shelling of December 13, 1862.

BATTLE OF FREDERICKSBURG DECEMBER 13, 1862

Following the Union victory at the Battle of Antietam in September 1862, at which Confederate General Robert E. Lee had been forced to abandon his attempted advance into Union territory, President Abraham Lincoln was anxious that Union Major General George B. McClellan should follow Lee into Virginia and cut the Confederate general off from his supply lines from the capital, Richmond. McClellan began to prepare the Army of the Potomac in October for the invasion of Virginia and set off in pursuit of Lee's Army of Northern Virginia, crossing the Potomac at the end of the month with his 120,000-strong army. However, his characteristic cautiousness caused him to advance only slowly and on 5 November the President's frustration at his slow progress led Lincoln to relieve McClellan and replace him with Major General Ambrose E. Burnside on the 9th.

Meanwhile, Lee was splitting his army in Virginia, dispatching Lieutenant General Thomas J. Jackson's corps to guard the Shenandoah Valley and Lieutenant General James Longstreet's corps east to block the route to Richmond. Burnside planned to aim directly for Richmond, bypassing Lee's forces in eastern Virginia and taking his army across the Rappahannock River at the town of Fredericksburg. If he could move fast enough he would be able to cross the river before Longstreet's forces arrived and the way to Richmond would then be open to him. Burnside also reorganized the Army of the Potomac into three wings, or "Grand Divisions"—the Right under Major General Edwin V. Sumner, the Center under Major General Joseph Hooker, and the Left under Major General William B. Franklin.

The Marye house, with rifle pits in front.

On November 15 Burnside and his army set off south towards the Rappahannock. Marching rapidly, the first Union troops reached the river at Fredericksburg on November 17. The speed of Burnside's advance took Lee by surprise and the town was only lightly defended, with Longstreet and his nearest corps over a day's march away. By November 20 Burnside's entire army had established itself on Stafford Heights, across the river from Fredericksburg, but there its advance halted. As expected, the Confederates had destroyed the bridges crossing the river and as the river was too wide and deep to ford, Burnside awaited the arrival of trains of pontoon boats on which his engineers were to build floating bridges. He had been promised by the War Department that the pontoon trains would be sent to Fredericksburg when he reached the river but in fact organizational problems in Washington meant that the first pontoons did not arrive until the 24th and the Union had lost the initiative.

The delay gave Lee time to rush Longstreet's corps to Fredericksburg, which it reached on November 21. Although this still gave him only 40,000 men to face Burnside's large army, the Confederates were in a strong position, dug-in on Marye's Heights, a high ridge immediately above the town, commanding the river. Events had overtaken Burnside's original plan and he appeared paralyzed as to the next move. Deciding he could not turn back or attempt a river crossing elsewhere, he belatedly gave the order for the pontoon bridges to be laid. His plan was to cross the river in two places. Sumner's Right Grand Division was to attack Fredericksburg directly across the river with Hooker's Center Grand Division crossing an adjacent bridge in support, while Franklin's Left Grand Division was to cross the river two miles downstream and outflank Lee on his right. On the evening of December 10 work started on the bridges—three bridges being constructed at each of the two crossing

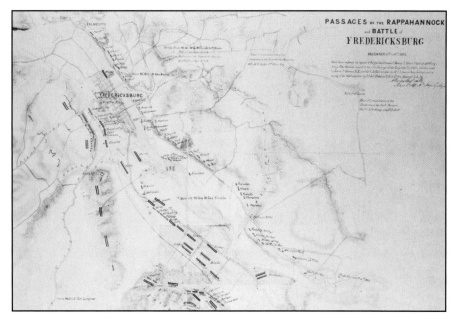

Map of the Battle of Fredericksburg.

points—but the local populace had evacuated the town and Confederate sharpshooters placed in buildings on the waterfront seriously hindered their progress, despite being shelled by the Union artillery.

From his vantage point high above the town and the river Lee could see exactly where the planned attack would come. He now had 70,000 men at his disposal as Jackson's corps had since arrived and Jackson was ordered to defend the southerly river crossing near Hamilton's Crossing while Longstreet's corps would hold Marye's Heights.

At Fredericksburg the constant Confederate fire meant that Sumner and Hooker did not get their forces across the river and into the town until late on December 12. Franklin had a much easier time downriver and completed his crossing the day before but then waited for the main attack before advancing further. On the morning of December 13 the Union troops attacked. In the south at 08:30 Franklin sent one division forward under Major General George G. Meade. This managed to break through a gap in Jackson's lines but as Franklin was unsure whether Burnside intended him to push on towards Lee and Longstreet or merely hold high ground in the south, the attack was only lightly supported and was driven back by a Confederate counterattack in the early afternoon. By 14:00 the fighting in the south died down with the positions in stalemate.

Meanwhile, in Fredericksburg Sumner had drawn up his men in the town awaiting the order from Burnside to attack. With no news of a successful advance by Franklin, Burnside finally ordered Sumner forward at midday. Longstreet's troops were well dug in, protected behind a stone wall, and their artillery fire followed by concerted fire from the infantry decimated the oncoming ranks of Union troops. Throughout

Portrait of Maj. Gen. Ambrose E. Burnside, commander of the Army of the Potomac.

the afternoon Sumner then Hooker's corps suffered huge casualties as they attacked Marye's Heights in waves across the open ground, before nightfall brought an end to the fighting. None had reached the stone wall and that evening Burnside was persuaded by his generals to abandon the attack, his army having suffered over 12,600 casualties, 8–10,000 of which fell on Marye's Heights, compared to Confederate losses of 5,377. Two days later Burnside pulled out of Fredericksburg, returning back across the Rappahannock.

PARTICIPATING UNITS:

Confederates: ....General Robert E. Lee, Army of Northern Virginia, 70,000

Union: ....Major General Ambrose B. Burnside, Army of the Potomac, 120,000

THE BATTLE:

Duration of battle:....One day; December 13, 1862

Location of battle:......Fredericksburg, Virginia

Outcome: ....Confederate victory

CASUALTY FIGURES:

Confederates: ....5,377 casualties; 603 killed, 4,116 wounded and remainder (approx 6-700) missing

Union: ....12,653 casualties; 1,284 killed, 9,600 wounded and 1,769 missing

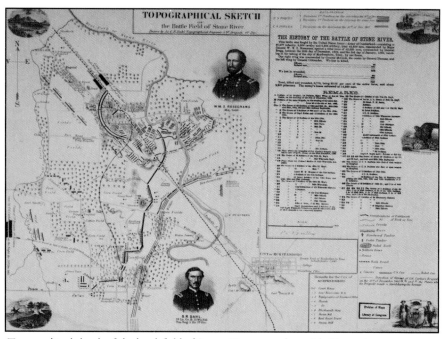

Topographical sketch of the battlefield of Stones River, complete with illustrations.

THE BATTLE OF STONES RIVER, DECEMBER 31, 1862–JANUARY 2, 1863

In terms of the percentage losses suffered by both sides during the war, the Battle of Stones River at Murfreesboro, in Tennessee was by far the bloodiest, with the Union forces under William Stark Rosecrans losing 31% of its troops and the Confederate Army of Tennessee, under Bragg, losing more than a third of its manpower.

On December 26, Rosecrans' Army of Cumberland departed from Nashville with a force of some 45,000 men. Facing him was Braxton Bragg with some 8,000 fewer infantrymen, but this imbalance was made up in part by the Confederate cavalry under Joseph Wheeler, a force that harried Rosecrans' advance but could not prevent the Union army approaching the Confederate army astride the Stones River. Both sides planned to attack on the morning of December 31, but it was Bragg who took the initiative, launching a major attack against the Union left, forcing it to retreat some three miles.

Faced by the need to defend his left flank, Rosecrans abandoned his own scheme to attack the Confederate left, and it was only staunch defense in the center by Philip Sheridan that prevented the day turning into a rout of the Union army. Sheridan's action, however, came at a high price as he lost almost one-third of his men killed or injured. With the Union defensive line now altered, Bragg identified the Round Forest as the pivotal point of the Union defense, ordering his forces, under John C. Breckinridge, to attack. By the end of the day's action, neither side could claim victory, although the balance appeared to have swung in the Confederate's favor.

The following day, January 1, 1863, saw relatively little action, although Union forces did capture a hill to the east of Stones River and

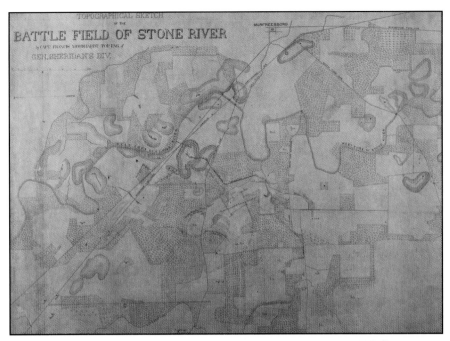

Map produced by an engineer on Gen. Sheridan's staff, showing the battlefield of Stones River.

it was this hill, the next day, that was to be the focus of Confederate action when the reluctant Breckinridge was ordered to take it. As he feared, although the Union troops were quickly removed, his own force, too, suffered heavy casualties. Bragg continued to see the battle as a Confederate victory and expected the Union forces to withdraw. However, come the morning of January 3 and with the Union forces still in place and on the point of being reinforced from Nashville, Bragg decided himself to withdraw. For both sides, Stones River proved indecisive: Bragg withdrew and Rosecrans deferred further action until the strength of his force was restored.

PARTICIPATING UNITS:

Confederates: .... General Braxton Bragg, Army of Tennessee, 37,000

Union: .... Major General William S. Rosecrans, Army of the Cumberland, 45,000

THE BATTLE:

Duration of battle: .... Three days; December 31, 1862–January 2, 1863

Location of battle: ..... Stones River at Murfreesboro, Tennessee

Outcome: .... Confederate victory

CASUALTY FIGURES:

Confederates: 10,266

Union: 13,249

Personnel in front of the Quartermaster's Office at Aquia Creek Landing, Va.

BATTLE OF CHANCELLORSVILLE MAY 2–3, 1863

Following his debacle at Fredericksburg and the subsequent abortive attempt to outflank General Robert E. Lee's army in January 1863 upstream of the Rappahannock, which had to be abandoned when the marching troops became bogged down in the mud, Ambrose E. Burnside resigned as commander of the Army of the Potomac. On January 25 President Lincoln replaced him with Major General Joseph Hooker.

During the next few months Hooker concentrated on collecting intelligence and rebuilding the morale of his army, still just across the Rappahannock River from Lee's Army of Northern Virginia, both armies in the positions they had adopted after the Battle of Fredericksburg. By April Hooker had formulated a plan for defeating Lee: he would cross the river with a large force 20 miles upstream at Kelley's Ford and march southeast on Lee, while the remainder of his army would be able to cross the river immediately north and south of Fredericksburg when Lee's attention was distracted, encircling the Confederates.

By April 26 Hooker's army had grown to 130,000 men and he set his plan in motion. He dispatched his cavalry corps led by Major General George Stoneman south to cut off Lee's communications with Richmond and divert the Confederate cavalry. The next day three infantry corps under Major Generals George G. Meade, Oliver O. Howard, and Henry W. Slocum started their march to Kelley's Ford. The majority of two further corps led by Major Generals Darius N. Couch and Daniel E. Sickles were to cross the river nearer upstream at United States' and Banks' Fords, while another corps led by Major General Joseph Reynolds was to cross the river downstream of Fredericksburg to cut off Lee's forces from Richmond to the south. Major General John Sedgwick remained at Fredericksburg with his corps to tie Lee's forces down at the town.

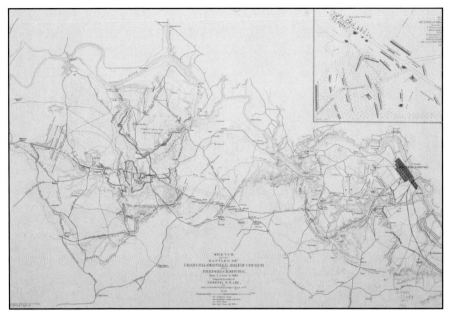

Sketch of the battles of Chancellorsville, Salem Church, and Fredericksburg. Over 30,000 would die in the battles.

As usual Lee faced a much larger army and he had further weakened his forces by sending Lieutenant General James Longstreet's corps to bolster Confederate forces in the Carolinas earlier in April, leaving him just 60,000 men at Fredericksburg. By April 30 Hooker's five corps had successfully crossed the river at the various designated fords and had collected in an area of dense scrub known as the "Wilderness" near Chancellorsville, 10 miles west of Fredericksburg. By this stage Lee had become aware of the extent of the Union troop movements to his rear, and gambling that Sedgwick's forces opposite Fredericksburg were a diversionary tactic, left just one division of 10,000 men under Major General Jubal A. Early to hold the town against Sedgwick's 47,000-strong corps while he pulled the majority of his forces out towards Chancellorsville to face Hooker on the 30th.

At this stage Hooker apparently lost his nerve. Having consolidated his forces at Chancellorsville he halted his advance party through the Wilderness on May 1 immediately he encountered Confederate skirmishers from Lieutenant General Thomas J. Jackson's corps and adopted instead a defensive position five miles long in the thick woods around Chancellorsville to wait for Lee's army, trusting that his superiority in numbers, 73,000 compared to Lee's 43,000, would carry the day. He expected the attack to come along the turnpike road to Chancellorsville and arranged his forces accordingly but Lee had received intelligence from his cavalry commander Major General James E. B. Stuart—whom he had not sent after the Union cavalry—that Hooker's far right flank, held by Howard's corps, was exposed and vulnerable to attack from the west. Lee sensed that Howard had gone on the defensive and was not about to launch an attack and took a further gamble to split his forces once more.

Lord Abinger (William F. Scarlett, 3d Baron Abinger, Lt. Col. Scots Fusilier Guards) and group at headquarters, Army of the Potomac, Falmouth, Va.

At 10:00 on May 2 Jackson took 32,000 men on a nine-mile circular march round Hooker's right flank, leaving Lee just 12,000 men to demonstrate against the Union force at Chancellorsville. During the day, while Lee engaged in troop movements and sporadic artillery fire on the Union line, Hooker received news of Jackson's movements and even a skirmish with Sickle's troops but interpreted them as a retreat. At 17:00 Jackson had organized his troops in the Wilderness and attacked Howard's men in the woods, along the Orange Turnpike. Howard was caught completely by surprise and his corps was overrun in 15 minutes. Jackson pressed on and Sickles' corps was next threatened with encirclement. The fighting continued into the night but by 20:00 Hooker had managed to stabilize his lines with the help of reinforcements from Reynold's corps, which had arrived across the Rappahannock River late that afternoon, into an L-shape against the Rappahannock and Rapidan Rivers. A serious setback to the Confederate cause occurred when Jackson rode forward to reconnoiter the road to continue the attack and was mistakenly fired on in the dark. The resulting wounds were fatal, Jackson dying eight days later, and the attack was called off for the night.

On the morning of May 3 Lee and Major General J. E. B. Stuart, who had taken command of Jackson's corps, renewed the Confederate attack on the Union salient, supported by massed artillery. The intense fighting lasted throughout the morning and in the absence of any news of Sedgwick at Fredericksburg Hooker ordered the Union troops to pull back towards the Rappahannock the afternoon. Sedgwick's orders had in fact been confused and he had only crossed the river into Fredericksburg late on May 2, launching his assault on Early's troops at 10:30 on May 3. He soon took Marye's Heights and was on his way toward Chancellorsville but as the fighting there had died down, Lee was

Gen. Ambrose E. Burnside and staff at the army's encampment at Warrenton.

able to detach a division to stop Sedgwick at the Battle of Salem Church on May 4, forcing him back across the Rappahannock. The next night Hooker also took his army back across the river. Overall, the Union had suffered almost 17,000 casualties compared to near 13,000 Confederate casualties and were no nearer defeating Lee or threatening Richmond. Yet the Confederate victory had come at cost, for Lee had lost his right-hand man, "Stonewall" Jackson.

PARTICIPATING UNITS:
Confederates: .... General Robert E. Lee, Army of Northern Virginia, 60,000
Union: .... Major General Joseph Hooker, Army of the Potomac, 130,000

THE BATTLE:
Duration of battle: .... Two days; May 2–3, 1863
Location of battle: ..... Chancellorsville, Virginia
Outcome: .... Confederate victory

CASUALTY FIGURES:
Confederates: 12,800
Union: 16,800

The 50th Pennsylvania Infantry in parade formation, Beaufort, S.C.

THE FIRST CONSCRIPTION ACT MARCH 1863

By 1863 recruitment for the Union was becoming a problem. The war economy was booming and the consequent reduction in unemployment meant that there were fewer available men to serve as volunteers in the army. In addition to the problems caused by economic growth, the Union also faced the imminent loss of servicemen coming to the end of their careers: by 1863 the men of 38 two-year regiments and of 92 nine-month militias were due to leave the army. Before the federal government took action, recruitment had been organized state by state, but only a federal act would allow for conscription. By the time that the Union states moved towards conscription, the Confederacy had already introduced it, the first of its three Conscription Acts being passed on April 16, 1862. The Union Congress passed the first of its Conscription Acts in March 1863. This allowed for the creation of a Provost Marshall Department within the War Department and for drafts to be undertaken in July 1863 and in March, July, and December 1864. Although, theoretically, the act opened the way to mass conscription of all males aged between 20 and 45, there were countless exclusions—those holding property, for example, could pay for others to take their place, while there were also exclusions for only sons, certain professions, and medical conditions. As a result the draft fell mainly on immigrants, such as the Irish in New York, and on those without the resources to acquire exemption. Moreover, many of the individual states sought to undermine the act through legal challenges and, for the volunteer soldiers, the new recruits were despised and regarded as inadequate in the face of battle. Elsewhere, those named in the draft often failed to report to duty.

The encampment at Beaufort, SC.

Provost Marshal General Marsena R. Patrick and staff, Culpeper, Va.

Six officers of the 17th New York Battery.

LEE'S INVASION OF THE NORTH JUNE 3, 1863

Having forestalled the latest Union campaign in Confederate Virginia at Chancellorsville, Confederate General Robert E. Lee was ready to renew his plan to take the war into Union territory in an attempt to force the Union to sue for peace. Strengthened by the return of Lieutenant General James Longstreet's corps in early May, Lee's Army of Northern Virginia now numbered 73,000 for his invasion of the North. His plan was to move up the Shenandoah Valley, using Major General James E. B. Stuart's 10,000-strong cavalry corps to screen his infantry and artillery movements from Major General Joseph Hooker's Army of the Potomac, still encamped in northern Virginia. Lee intended to cross the Potomac River north of the Shenandoah Valley and enter Maryland then Pennsylvania before Hooker could react.

On June 3, 1863, Lee's army left Fredericksburg to march into the Shenandoah Valley. Receiving intelligence of Confederate movements at Culpeper, although not suspecting a major invasion, Hooker dispatched his cavalry corps of 11,000 men under Brigadier General Alfred Pleasonton. At Brandy Station on June 9 Pleasonton surprised Stuart. In what would be the largest cavalry engagement of the war, Stuart eventually drove off Pleasonton, but during the fighting the Union cavalry had matched the Confederates for the first time. Stuart's consequent desire to re-establish his ascendancy would have a significant impact on Lee's forthcoming campaign.

The encounter spurred Lee on to move his men quickly into the Shenandoah Valley in the following week. En route to Sharpsburg Lieutenant General Richard S. Ewell's corps captured a Union garrison at Winchester on June 14, while first Lieutenant General James Longstreet's then Major General Ambrose P. Hill's corps followed up the east side of

Portrait of Maj. Gen. Joseph Hooker, who would meet Lee at Gettysburg.

the valley. By now Hooker realized that Lee was moving his army toward Union territory. Although he set off north in pursuit, Lee had stolen a march on him and the Confederates were able to cross the Potomac on June 23 to enter Union territory—Maryland—by late June. At this point, on June 25, Lee acceded to Stuart's request to take the cavalry in a sweeping raid to harass Hooker's rear, cutting off his supply lines to Washington. Although the raid was a success, the distance between the two armies meant that Lee would have to operate in enemy territory without the benefit of the intelligence normally supplied by his cavalry.

Lee continued his advance through Maryland, toward Pennsylvania, with Ewell's corps leading. Although Hooker now moved quickly, crossing the Potomac on June 26 and reaching Frederick late on the 27th, the pressure of events caused Hooker to resign his command that evening. He was replaced the same night by Major General George G. Meade. Within days he was to meet Lee's army where it had converged at Gettysburg in one of the defining battles of the war.

Levee and steamboats at Vicksburg, Miss.

UNION ADVANCE ON VICKSBURG NOVEMBER 1862–JULY 1863

In the west in the latter part of 1862, Union advances threatened to split Confederate territory in two along the Mississippi. In October Major General Ulysses S. Grant assumed command of the Army of the Tennessee and his key objective became the heavily fortified Confederate city of Vicksburg on the eastern bank of the Mississippi River. Shortly afterward, the Confederates replaced their commander of the Army of the Mississippi, Major General Earl Van Dorn, with Lieutenant General John C. Pemberton, one of whose first tasks was to strengthen the defenses at Vicksburg.

Grant quickly moved his army to Grand Junction on the Mississippi border, where he built up supplies for his strike through enemy territory at Vicksburg. He planned to coordinate his advance with an assault on Vicksburg down the river by a corps led by Brigadier General William T. Sherman, which was temporarily placed by President Lincoln under the overall command of the Democrat politician John McClernand. Grant started to move his troops south in November, pausing at Holly Springs to establish a supply base. Pemberton, realizing that he was outnumbered (22,000 Confederates facing Grant's 40,000 men), pulled back to Grenada and called for reinforcements. However, a dramatic attack by Van Dorn, now in command of Pemberton's cavalry, forced Grant to abandon his advance. On December 20 Van Dorn destroyed Grant's supply base at Holly Springs while another Confederate cavalry detachment led by Brigadier General Nathan B. Forrest severed Grant's supply lines further north at Jackson.

It was too late for Grant to get word of these setbacks to Sherman, who was on his way down the Mississippi with his 32,000 troops, and Sherman's attack on Chickasaw Bluffs, just north of Vicksburg,

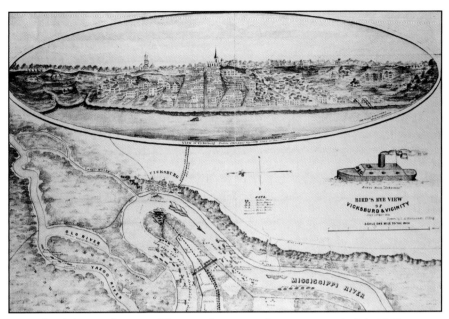

Map of Vicksburg and vicinity. This map shows an earlier engagement in July 1862.

on December 27 ended in failure. The Confederates had been able to concentrate their forces at Vicksburg and Sherman's men suffered heavy losses in the assault on the well-defended heights, retreating back up the river.

Although McClernand took the credit for another Union attack down the Mississippi, when Sherman and Commander David D. Porter of the U.S. Navy took Fort Hindman in Arkansas from the Confederates in January 1863, the problems caused by a split command led Grant to take overall control of the operations against Vicksburg on January 30. He decided to continue the campaign against the city from the river, on the west of the city, where his 60,000-strong army was encamped.

During the wet winter months Grant surveyed the possible weak points of the Confederate fortress. A direct assault was too risky because of the firepower of the Confederate batteries dominating the river crossing; the same was true on the high ground to the north of Vicksburg. This left the more open land to the south and east of the city as the best attack route. However, to get there he had to maneuver his men downriver past the massed Confederate batteries lining the cliffs along the river. After several fruitless expeditions to determine if there was a way through the swamps and bayous surrounding the Union encampment, and even to build a canal which would take his troops far enough downriver out of the reach of the batteries, Grant decided on a plan of action. While his army would march south through the marshes on the west bank of the Mississippi, aided by shallow-draught transports, Porter would take the gunboats of the Mississippi River Squadron to ferry the troops across the Mississippi some 60–70 miles downriver of Vicksburg.

Rear Admiral David D. Porter and staff aboard his flagship, U.S.S. Malvern, *Hampton Roads, Va.*

At the start of April Grant sent two corps under Major Generals John A. McClernand and James B. McPherson to start their march through the marshes. On the night of April 16 Porter's flotilla started to sail downstream past Vicksburg. Despite being pounded by the batteries his ships reached the designated crossing place at Bruinsburg with minimal losses. On April 30–May 1 the 43,000 men of McClernand's and McPherson's command crossed the river virtually unopposed as the Confederates' attention had been distracted by diversionary attacks by Sherman's corps at Vicksburg and a cavalry raid led by Brigadier General Benjamin H. Grierson through the state of Mississippi. Although Pemberton sent a detachment from Vicksburg in an attempt to stop Grant, this was brushed aside at Fort Gibson on May 1 before Grant moved on to occupy the Grand Gulf garrison then take the Mississippi capital of Jackson on May 14. Pemberton, realizing the precariousness of his position, requested reinforcements before taking his forces outside Vicksburg to avoid being trapped in the city.

As Grant's forces turned towards Vicksburg, Pemberton attempted to halt the Union advance on the morning of May 16 at Champions Hill. Although outnumbered, with only 23,000 men at his disposal, Pemberton established himself in a strong position east of the Big Black River and achieved some success early in the battle against McClernand's and McPherson's corps, but was driven back by midafternoon with heavy losses. The Confederates returned to their prepared defenses at Vicksburg on May 19, to prepare for the siege from Grant.

Twice Grant launched assaults against the fortifications—on May 19 and 22—but, although his army had been reinforced with the arrival of Sherman's corps, he was beaten back with the loss of 3,200 men. However, the shortage of food, constant artillery barrage, and lack of relieving troops forced Pemberton to surrender the garrison on 4 July, cutting the Confederacy in two.

Portrait of Maj. Gen. James B. McPherson.

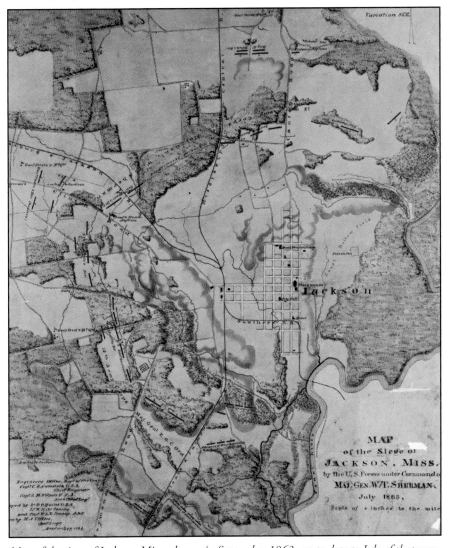

Map of the siege of Jackson, Miss., drawn in September 1863, up to date to July of that year.

BATTLE OF MILLIKEN'S BEND JUNE 7, 1863

The Battle of Milliken's Bend, Louisiana was part of Grant's operation against Vicksburg. The Union forces, commanded by Colonel Hermann Lieb, consisted of the African Brigade and the 23rd Iowa Volunteer Infantry. Facing them was a Confederate division commanded by Brigadier General Henry E. McCulloch. Early on June 6, Lieb with the African Brigade and two companies from the 10th Illinois Cavalry, reconnoitered the area towards Richmond, Louisiana. However, some three miles from the town Lieb's forces came face to face with Confederate troops at Tallulah, forcing the latter to retreat. Rather than follow the Confederates, Lieb withdrew, being uncertain if their forces were being reinforced. He withdrew to Milliken's Bend, where he established a defensive position and relayed information concerning the day's actions to his commanders. Two gunboats—the Lexington and the Choctaw—and the 23rd Iowa Infantry were dispatched to support him before Confederate forces arrived. McCulloch's troops arrived at 03:00 the following morning, and despite fire from Union guns, attacked the Union left flank, causing significant casualties. The Union force was gradually pushed back toward the river where the presence of the gunboats proved decisive. Although the Confederates continued to press forward, the Union line held and the Confederate forces withdrew

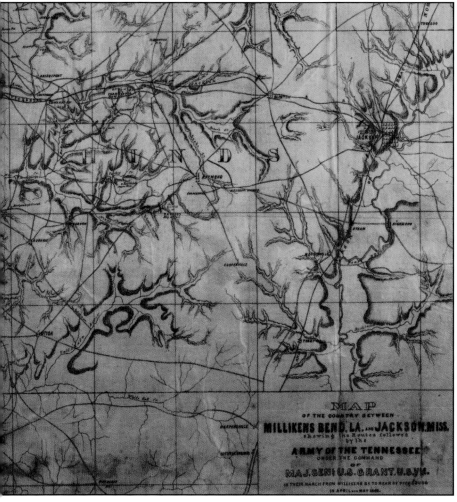

Map of Millikens Bend, La, and Jackson, Miss.

towards Walnut Bayou at about noon under continued fire from the gunboats. While the engagement was a Union success, in terms of casualties, the Union lost more.

PARTICIPATING UNITS:

Confederates: .... Brigadier General Henry E. McCulloch's brigade

Union: .... Colonel Hermann Lieb, African Brigade and the 23rd Iowa Volunteer Infantry

THE BATTLE:

Duration of battle: .... Two days; May 2–3, 1863

Location of battle: ..... Madison's Parish, Louisiana

Outcome: .... Union victory

CASUALTY FIGURES:

Confederates: 185

Union: 652

The Bryan house on IInd Corps' line, near the scene of Pickett's Charge.

BATTLE OF GETTYSBURG JULY 1–3, 1863

Confederate General Robert E. Lee's invasion of Union territory for the second time in the war, in June 1863, was to culminate in the most famous battle of the conflict. As his Army of Northern Virginia entered Pennsylvania, the pursuing Union Army of the Potomac, newly under the command of Major General George G. Meade, began to close him down until the two armies converged on the small crossroads town of Gettysburg.

News of the proximity of Meade's army forced Lee to abandon his plan to cross the Susquehanna River and continue his invasion of the North. His leading forces, Lieutenant General Richard S. Ewell's corps, had actually reached the river but on June 28 Lee ordered them to pull back to Gettysburg, where the remainder of his army would concentrate to face the Union army at his rear.

The first troops to arrive at Gettysburg—on June 30—were two advance Union cavalry brigades led by Brigadier General John Buford, who dug in on the slopes of McPherson's Ridge, intending to delay the Confederate advance until the nearest Union infantry corps led by Major General John F. Reynolds could reach them. That afternoon a Confederate patrol ran into Buford's troops and when the news of the Union troops at Gettysburg reached Lee's leading corps commander, Major General Ambrose P. Hill, his most advanced division, under Major General Henry Heth, readied itself for attack the next morning.

Heth's division set off towards the town at dawn and reached the defensive positions of Buford's cavalry at 08:00. Although outnumbered, the Union troops managed to hold out for two hours, long enough to delay the Confederate advance until the arrival of Reynold's infantry on the ridge.

Bodies of Confederate soldiers, killed on July 1, collected near the McPherson woods.

As more units were sucked in, what had originally been intended as a skirmish began to turn into a major battle, but one in which events were overtaking Lee's plans. Although Reynolds was killed by a chance bullet, his men reinforced the line under their new commander, Major General Abner Doubleday, and Heth, finding he was up against more Union troops than expected, required reinforcements from the remainder of Hill's forces from the west. At the same time, around midday, the next Union corps under Major General Oliver O. Howard arrived on the battlefield and took up position on the ridge to the right of Doubleday.

Despite the heavy Confederate attacks, the Union forces continued to hold their positions when Lee reached the battlefield at 14:00. Seeing larger than expected numbers of Union infantry, he considered whether to pull back when Ewell's corps arrived on the battlefield from the northeast at 15:00 and drove into the Union right wing. The Confederates' superiority in numbers at this stage, outflanking the Union troops, finally forced the Union lines back and Doubleday's wing collapsed. Seeing this success, Lee decided to press home his advantage as the Union troops retreated through the streets of Gettysburg.

South of the town was Cemetery Hill, on which a fresh Union brigade, led up from the south by Major General Winfield S. Hancock, was establishing defensive positions. The fleeing Union troops rallied round Hancock and in spite of the danger that the Union troops would establish themselves on the hill, with more reinforcements to come, Ewell did not renew the attack. The fighting died down on the first day around 17:30.

Dead Confederate soldiers in "the devil's den."

During the evening reinforcements arrived for both sides. For the Union, first Major General Daniel E. Sickles' then Major General Henry W. Slocum's corps arrived from the south before Meade himself reached the battlefield at 02:00. Judging Cemetery Hill to be a good defensive position, Meade arranged his troops along the ridge in a line three miles long. Running roughly north to south were Slocum's corps holding the right flank against Ewell at Culp's Hill, Howard and Hancock's corps on Cemetery Hill, with Sickles' corps forming a salient in the line on low ground in front of the ridge. Still to come was Sykes' corps, which would hold the Round Top group of hills at the southern end of the line.

Lee's army had also been strengthened during the night by the arrival of Lieutenant General James Longstreet's corps from the west. Although he now faced superior numbers—on the second day of the battle the Confederates numbered 50,000 and the Union 60,000—Lee decided to continue the attack. He judged the Union positions in the north to be too strong so decided to use Longstreet's fresh men in an attack on the south of the Union line, where Sickles was exposed, while Hill's and Ewell's corps would hold the rest of the line north. Much of the day was taken with moving two of Longstreet's divisions under Major Generals Lafayette McLaw and John B. Hood, and Longstreet only launched his assault at 16:00. Following an artillery barrage Hood attacked first, through a boulder-strewn area which became known as the "Devil's Den," followed by McLaw's division an hour later through a peach orchard and a wheat field. The Confederates managed to reach the high ground on Little Round Top but were pushed back by the arrival of Sykes' men, ending in a fierce hand-to-hand struggle in Devil's Den. In the fighting Sickles' corps was virtually annihilated but the Union line had not been broken and Longstreet's men were spent.

Dead Confederate soldiers in the "slaughter pen" at the foot of Little Round Top.

The Confederate attack also moved further up the line that afternoon. Hill attacked Hancock's position on Cemetery Hill with two divisions under Major General Richard H. Anderson, but again was beaten back from the ridge. At the north end, Ewell waited until 18:30 before attacking and by nightfall, despite breaking though the Union line in one place, was forced to call a halt to the fighting.

In spite of heavy losses—both sides suffering around 10,000 casualties that day—during the night Meade resolved to continue holding the ridge against Lee, guessing correctly that the Confederates would try another assault the next day. With more fresh troops arriving in the night—Major General George E. Pickett's division and Major General James E. B. Stuart's cavalry—Lee planned a frontal attack on the center of the Union line. Meade had also been able to strengthen his army overnight, Major General John Sedgwick's corps reinforcing his far left wing.

The first action on July 3 took place on the northern end of the line at 04:00, when Slocum attacked Ewell's men attempting to establish themselves on Culp Hill. By 10:30 the Confederates had been driven back, ensuring that the entire length of the ridge was again in Union hands. Having tried Meade's flanks, Lee then prepared for his massive central assault on Union lines. Longstreet lined up approximately 13,000 men for a concerted attack up Cemetery Ridge—Pickett would command his division of Virginians plus two divisions from Hill's corps, led by Brigadier General James J. Pettigrew, who had taken over from Heth when he was injured.

At 13:00 the Confederate artillery opened an immense barrage against Union positions on Cemetery Hill which lasted for two hours.

Headquarters of Gen. George G. Meade on Cemetery Ridge.

The Union guns replied but by 15:00 both sets of artillery were silent, and Longstreet launched his attack.

The Confederate infantry led by Pickett marched in formation across the open ground toward Cemetery Ridge into a wall of fire—first from the Union artillery then from the well-placed Union infantry. Thousands of Confederates fell in the attack, although a handful reached the Union guns on the crest of the hill before they were driven back. As the remnants of the massed attack streamed back Lee attempted to reorganize them in preparation for an anticipated counterattack by Meade but the Union troops remained on the ridge.

The next day both battered armies faced each other before Lee admitted defeat and withdrew his force back towards the Potomac and Virginia, that night. The bloodiest battle of the war had claimed 20,000 Confederate casualties and 23,000 Union casualties; although Meade's army was too exhausted to pursue Lee, it marked the end of Confederate ambitions to bring the war to the North.

Headquarters of Gen. Robert E. Lee on the Chambersburg Pike.

John L. Burns, the 69-year-old "hero of Gettysburg," with gun and crutches, who became a northern hero after picking up his flintlock and taking his place on the firing line.

The cemetery gatehouse.

Interior view of breastworks on extreme left of the Federal line

The center of the Federal position viewed from Little Round Top

G.J. White's house near Gettysburg.

PARTICIPATING UNITS:

Confederates: .... General Robert E. Lee, Army of Northern Virginia, 50,000 (third day)

Union: .... Major General George G. Meade, Army of the Potomac, 72,000 (third day)

THE BATTLE:

Duration of battle: .... Three days; July 1–3, 1863
Location of battle: ..... Gettysburg, Pennsylvania
Outcome: .... Union victory

CASUALTY FIGURES:

Confederates: .... 2,600-4,500 killed, 12,800 wounded, 5,250 missing, total casualties 20,650–28,000

Union: .... 3,155 killed, 14,530 wounded, 5,365 missing, total casualties 23,040

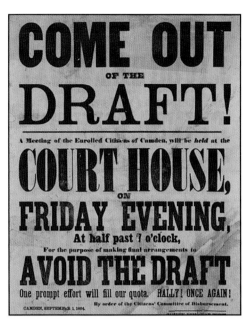

A Civil War draft poster

DRAFT RIOTS JULY 1863

During the early summer of 1863 tension in many northern towns and cities grew: the powder keg exploded on the streets of New York in the middle of July. In the period preceding this, there had been trouble in many urban areas, but it was in New York where the problems became most severe. There were a number of factors behind this—some religious, some economic—that resulted in the rioting that occurred between July 13 and 16. Much of the urban poor, Irish Catholic by ancestry, feared that the incoming blacks would undermine their position by taking the unskilled jobs and forcing wage rates down; already, the poor had suffered severely as a result of wages falling behind prices by some 20 percent since 1861. There were also overtones of a class struggle, with resentment against the predominantly Protestant middle and upper classes in the city.

Even before the riots, there had been a number of strikes, such as that of the longshoremen in June 1863, but the final straw came with the arrival of the draft officers on Saturday, July 11. The city was deprived of most of its military, sent to help the pursuit of Lee after Gettysburg, and so, when on July 12, the seeds of rioting were sewn in local bars, the authorities had no response when the rioting started on Monday, July 13. While there was some looting, much of the activity involved attacks on the houses of noted Republicans and pro-Republican newspapers; the offices of, for example, the New York Tribune were attacked. Also victims were those unfortunate blacks caught and lynched, as well as institutions, such as the Colored Orphan Asylum, that were attacked. That there were also economic and religious overtones to the riots was demonstrated by the fact that machinery, such as grain-loading elevators, and Protestant churches also fell victim to the mob.

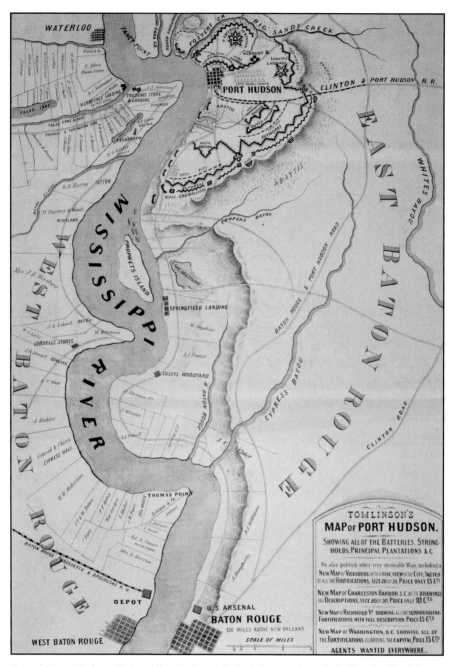

Map of Port Hudson. Besieged for 48 days, bloody fighting only ended when the Confederate commander, Major General Franklin Gardner, heard that Vicksburg had surrendered. On July 9, 1863, Port Hudson was opened to the Union forces.

The police proved ineffective and the small number of troops available were also overwhelmed. The authorities moved quickly, bringing regiments in from Pennsylvania. On July 15 and 16 these troops opened fire on the rioters with the result that, by July 17, an uneasy peace had been restored to the city. The authorities, however, took no chances when the next draft was due to take place: on August 19 some 20,000 troops were stationed in the city when the draft officers next sought to fulfil their quota.

The Battle of Honey Springs—the Gettysburg of the west—was the single most important battle fought on Indian territory during the course of the Civil War. It was also the single most important battle fought involving Native Americans, with both sides having soldiers from the Indian tribes. The battle was fought as both sides sought to control the Indian territory that now forms part of the state of Oklahoma. The Confederate army, under the command of General Douglas Cooper, was faced by Union army under the command of General James Blunt. Part of the Union army was formed of the 1st Kansas Colored Infantry; this was an all-black regiment that had come to prominence when it had defeated the Confederate forces at Cabin Creek in late June 1863.

The Confederate force, mainly comprising men from Texas, attacked early on the morning of July 17; opposing them were Indian troops allied to the Union. The Union plan was for these troops to retreat, thereby drawing the Confederate forces onto the guns of the 1st Kansas Regiment and, in this, the plan worked well. Realizing that his soldiers were taking casualties, Cooper ordered a withdrawal southward. Having gained a tactical advantage, the Union forces pressed forward pursuing the retreating Confederates for more than a mile before exhaustion set in. Although the Confederates were defeated, the inability of the Union army to press home its advantage meant that the remaining Confederate forces were able to withdraw intact.

PARTICIPATING UNITS:

Confederates: .... Brigadier General Douglas H. Cooper, 1st Brigade, Native American troops, 6,000

Union: .... Major General James G. Blunt, District of the Frontier, 3,000

THE BATTLE:

Duration of battle: .... One day; July 17, 1863

Location of battle: ..... Muskogee and McIntosh counties, Oklahoma

Outcome: .... Union victory

CASUALTY FIGURES:

Confederates: 637

Union: 79

Fort Wagner, Folly Island, South Carolina.

FORT WAGNER JULY 18, 1863

Located close to Charleston harbor, Fort Wagner was an earthen fortification held by the Confederate forces in defense of the port. On July 18, 1863, two Union brigades attacked the fort. The assault was led by the 54th Massachusetts Infantry commanded by Colonel Robert Gould Shaw. Although there was, theoretically, nothing unusual in such an action, this regiment was the Union's showcase regiment formed of black soldiers and it was also the regiment's first action. Shaw had persuaded his commanders to allow the regiment to be at the forefront of the assault and, while the defenders ultimately retained control of the fort, the remarkable bravery evinced by many of the black soldiers, some of whom briefly held the fort's parapet, was a useful counterpoint to the more negative news coming from within the Union states at a time of the draft riots. Of the regiment, almost half were killed and injured, including Colonel Shaw himself. The prominence given to the action was reflected in newspaper reports of the time: the New York Tribune, for example, commented that the engagement "made Fort Wagner such a name to the colored race as Bunker Hill had been for ninety years to the white Yankees." A campaign to have Shaw's body removed from the field and reburied away from his black soldiers failed, Shaw's father himself leading the campaign to ensure that the body remained with his soldiers, commenting "We hold that a soldier's most appropriate burial-place is on the field where he has fallen."

Garrison of Fort Wagner on parade.

Interior of Fort Wagner showing officers' quarters.

Right: Map showing Charleston Harbor and its approaches.

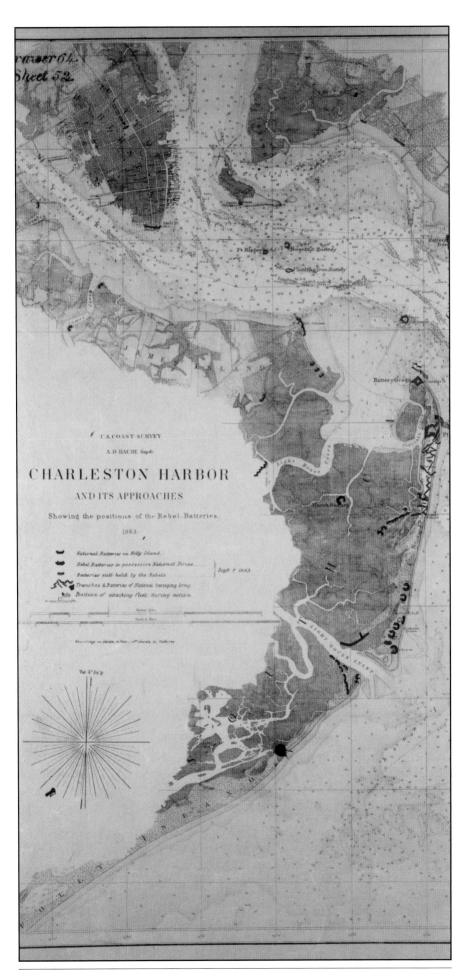

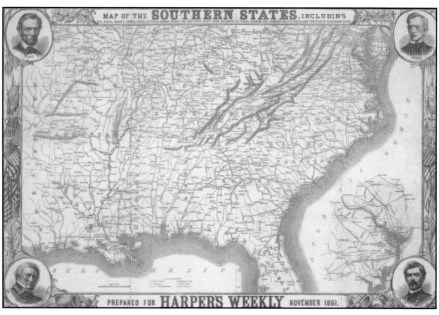

Map of the Southern states.

QUANTRILL RAID ON LAWRENCE AUGUST 21, 1863

In a war noted for the ferocity of many of its actions, among the most unpleasant of all activity occurred on the Missouri/Kansas border where guerrilla groups, effectively sanctioned by the Confederates (the Border Ruffians) and the Union (the Jayhawkers), fought a bloody war. In Missouri, the Union authorities sought to defeat the guerrillas by endeavoring to prevent the civilian population assisting them, but this had the effect of turning many into rebel sympathizers. Both sides in this struggle were ruthless, killing prisoners in cold blood and not differentiating between civilian and military populations.

Once of the most notorious guerrilla leaders was William Clarke Quantrill, a drifter before the war who was the son of an Ohio schoolteacher. Never pro-slavery as such, he was antipathetic towards blacks and authority and, in the service of the Confederate forces, he was able to wage war on both. In August 1862 a force led by Quantrill captured and pillaged the town of Independence, Missouri, which resulted in him being granted a commission in the Confederate army; it also enraged the Union commanders who sought to defeat him. As part of this policy, 14 wives and sisters of men within Quantrill's group were captured and imprisoned in Kansas City. Five were killed on August 14, 1863, when the roof of the prison collapsed and, vowing revenge, Quantrill led a group of 450 guerrillas against the city of Lawrence in Kansas. The guerillas captured 10 farmers en route as guides: they were killed as their usefulness ceased. Quantrill's forces entered the town on August 21, massacring 183 men and boys and destroying 185 buildings. A force of Union cavalry managed to force them to retreat, but 65 cavalrymen were killed at Baxters Spring during the chase. Although Quantrill escaped capture at this stage, a number of his followers were captured and executed. Quantrill himself was to be killed in 1865 when captured by Union troops while on a mission to assassinate Lincoln.

Umbrella Rock on Lookout Mountain.

BATTLE OF CHICKAMAUGA SEPTEMBER 1863

In summer 1863, the war in the west reached a crucial phase. As the siege at Vicksburg was reaching its climax, the campaign in Tennessee came to life again after six months of quiet. Following the Battle of Stones River (Murfreesboro), December 31, 1862–January 2, 1863, Union Major General William S. Rosecrans had rested his Army of the Cumberland in the area, while the Confederate Army of Tennessee under General Braxton Bragg had regrouped further south in Tennessee.

In June Rosecrans started to move in pursuit of Bragg, who pulled his forces into the strategically vital railroad junction of Chattanooga. Rosecrans then took his army across the Tennessee to the west of Chattanooga in August, outflanking Bragg, who evacuated the city, leaving the way open for Rosecrans to enter on September 9.

Rosecrans, mistakenly believing that Bragg's army was in full retreat, left one corps under Brigadier General Thomas L. Crittenden to hold Chattanooga and set off in pursuit with his other two corps, led by Major Generals Alexander M. McCook and George H. Thomas, which were allowed to separate to follow their own route through the mountains. By the first week in September Rosecrans' army was spread out over a 40-mile front across mountainous terrain.

In fact, not only was Bragg in tight control of his army, but he was also expecting reinforcements: 9,000 men of Major General Simon B. Buckner's corps from east Tennessee and two divisions of Lieutenant General James Longstreet's corps from Lee's army in Virginia. This would bring the number of men under Bragg's command to 60,000, which would give him numerical parity against Rosecrans' force, allowing him to concentrate superior forces against the isolated Union corps in turn.

Map of the Chickamauga battlefield. A Cherokee word, Chickamauga means "River of Death."

The mountainous terrain had screened Bragg's movements from Rosecrans so it was quite by chance that one of Thomas' divisions stumbled on Bragg's entire army on September 9 but vacillation on the part of Bragg allowed the division to escape. Rosecrans belatedly realized the imminent danger of his position and ordered his corps, including Crittenden, to converge at Chickamauga Creek, 12 miles south of Chattanooga. Two days later, further confusion over Bragg's orders to corps commanders allowed Crittenden's corps to escape being enveloped at its encampment along the creek, at Lee and Gordon's Mills.

For five days Bragg delayed his attack, allowing Thomas and McCook time to march north in support. The furthest troops had to march over 50 miles but by the 18th Rosecrans was able arrange his three corps in a line along the west bank of the Chickamauga, blocking the main route north to Chattanooga. Bragg's plan was to cross the Chickamauga and

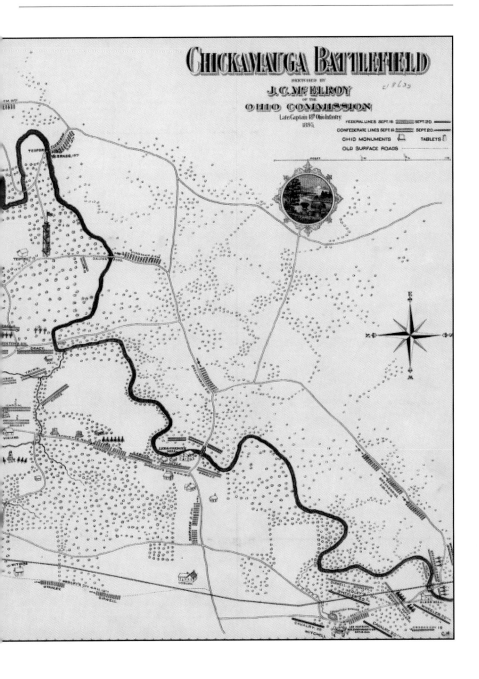

attack the Union left flank, turn it, and take the road to Chattanooga, isolating the Union army.

The battle started almost inadvertently in dense woods which masked enemy positions. On the morning of September 19, about 09:00, Thomas sent two divisions forward following information that a Confederate brigade was isolated on the Union side of the Chickamauga; instead, they encountered Brigadier General Nathan B. Forrest's dismounted cavalry corps, supported by one of Major General John B. Hood's divisions, led by Brigadier General Bushrod R. Johnson. The fighting quickly intensified, drawing in additional troops from both sides. The Confederate reserve corps led by Major General William H. T. Walker entered the battlefield and Thomas' corps began to be pushed back towards the Lafayette Road, but the Union lines stabilized.

The battle became chaotic as it spread along the line and commands became muddled—Bragg and Rosecrans both struggled to maintain a semblance of order. By midday it became apparent at the north of the battle that the Confederates were not going to break through Thomas' line to reach the Lafayette Road. Bragg, therefore, concentrated instead on attacks on the center of the line, but again failed to break through and the fighting died down at around 16:00.

That afternoon Longstreet's corps arrived on the battlefield, and Hood's corps launched a final assault that day on the Union lines, which continued to hold the road. By nightfall the battlefield was quiet and the two commanders discussed their relative situations with their subordinates. Rosecrans decided to hold his positions, but Bragg decided to reorganize his army into two wings, the left under Longstreet—Hood's corps, Buckner's corps, and Major General Thomas C. Hindman's division—and the right under Lieutenant General Leonidas Polk, with Walkers' corps, Hill's corps, and Major General Benjamin F. Cheatham's division. Bragg planned to attack the next day, starting with Polk, who would push the Union force away from the Lafayette Road before Longstreet administered the final blow.

Polk's attack on the morning of September 20 did not start until 09:30 but the ferocity of the fighting was such that Thomas was forced to request Rosecrans to send him reinforcements. Brigadier General Thomas J. Wood was ordered to redeploy his division from the center to the Union left wing but his movement left a wide gap in the lines. Longstreet saw his opportunity and launched a massive attack at midday with his five divisions, breaking through the Union lines and splitting their army in two. McCook's and Crittenden's corps collapsed, the men fleeing the battlefield, but Thomas on the left wing stood firm, earning himself the nickname "The Rock of Chickamauga." Although attacked on three sides by Longstreet's and Polk's forces, Thomas' men managed to hold out until nightfall on Snodgrass Hill and Horseshoe Ridge, when, with the assistance of Brigadier General Gordon Granger's reserve corps, they were able to retreat from the battlefield as Bragg decided not to pursue them.

It had been a costly battle, the Confederates suffering 18,500 casualties and the Union 16,000, but although the Confederates had won the day, Thomas' heroic stand enabled the Union army to escape total destruction and Chattanooga was still in Union hands.

Portrait of Maj. Gen. George H. Thomas.

PARTICIPATING UNITS:
Confederates: .... General Braxton Bragg, Army of Tennessee, 60,000
Union: .... Major General William S. Rosecrans, Army of the
Cumberland, 60,000

THE BATTLE:
Duration of battle: .... Two days; September 19–20, 1863
Location of battle: ..... Chickamauga Creek, Georgia
Outcome: .... Confederate victory

CASUALTY FIGURES:
Confederates: 18,500
Union: 16,000

GETTYSBURG ADDRESS

Lincoln's Gettysburg Address is inscribed on the south wall of his Washington memorial.

The Battle of Gettysburg in July 1863 was seen as a turning point in the Civil War, even at the time. It was to be the bloodiest battle of the conflict, and General Robert E. Lee's defeat marked the end of Confederate ambitions to mount a major offensive on Union territory, to force recognition of the breakaway states.

In November of that year President Lincoln traveled to the Pennsylvanian town of Gettysburg to take part in the dedication ceremony for the new cemetery for the soldiers who had died in the battle. The President arrived on a special train the night before the dedication ceremony, and the next day, November 19, 1863, he rode through the town to the cemetery on the site of the battlefield. Lincoln did not give the main address at the ceremony; that honor had been given to a noted orator of the day, Edward Everett. Everett's speech lasted two hours and by the time Lincoln came to say his words the attention of the 10–15,000-strong crowd had begun to wander. Lincoln's speech was short—less than 300 words, lasting two minutes. Many in the crowd missed it and the official photographer was not quick enough to record the event, but the Gettysburg Address has subsequently become regarded as an eloquent summary of the war, being later inscribed on the wall of the Lincoln memorial and today learned by schoolchildren throughout the United States.

Several myths surround the Gettysburg Address, one of which is that Lincoln wrote the address on the back of an envelope as he traveled on the train to Gettysburg. In fact, a number of drafts exist from before and after the address, showing that Lincoln meticulously crafted the speech for an audience which would look beyond the war. Invoking the language of another great text of American history, the Declaration of Independence, he deliberately refrained from divisive references to the civil war and the Union, instead stressing the unity of the entire nation, inclusive of all.

"Fourscore and seven years ago our fathers brought forth on this continent a new nation, conceived in liberty and dedicated to the proposition that all men are created equal.

Now we are engaged in a great civil war, testing whether that nation or any nation so conceived and so dedicated can long endure. We are met on a great battlefield of that war. We have come to dedicate a portion of it as a final resting place for those who died here that the nation might live. This we may, in all propriety do. But in a larger sense, we cannot dedicate, we cannot consecrate, we cannot hallow this ground. The brave men, living and dead who struggled here have hallowed it far above our poor power to add or detract. The world will little note nor long remember what we say here, but it can never forget what they did here.

It is rather for us the living, we here be dedicated to the great task remaining before us—that from these honored dead we take increased devotion to that cause for which they here gave the last full measure of devotion—that we here highly resolve that these dead shall not have died in vain, that this nation shall have a new birth of freedom, and that government of the people, by the people, for the people shall not perish from the earth."

Confederate prisoners at railroad depot, Chattanooga, Tenn.

BATTLE OF CHATTANOOGA NOVEMBER 23–25, 1863

Following the rout of his Union forces at the Battle of Chickamauga, Major General William S. Rosecrans retreated with his Army of the Cumberland to the safety of Chattanooga in September 1863. There he awaited a Confederate assault as the town of Chattanooga, on the Tennessee River, was a strategically vital railroad junction giving east-west access into the Confederacy.

Three days after Chickamauga, on September 23, Confederate Major General Braxton Bragg set off in pursuit of Rosecrans at Chattanooga. There his Army of Tennessee occupied the heights around the city to lay siege to the Union troops.

Rosecrans was in a precarious position, and his political masters knew it. President Lincoln and General Henry W. Halleck at the War Department in Washington ordered that two corps under the command of Major General Joseph Hooker be detached from the Army of the Potomac to reinforce Rosecrans' army. They also created a new command, the Military Division of the Mississippi, putting Major General Ulysses S. Grant in overall command at Chattanooga. Unimpressed with Rosecrans' record, Grant replaced him with Major General George H. Thomas, who had performed so heroically at Chickamauga.

On October 23 Grant himself visited Chattanooga and found the Army of the Cumberland in a sorry state. Bragg's troops on Lookout Mountain had cut off the Union's main supply route along the Tennessee River, as well as the roads and rail routes leading into the city. Only one wagon road through the mountains remained partially open. His immediate priority was to open a supply line and on October 27

U.S. military train at Chattanooga depot; Lookout Mountain in background.

Brigadier General William F. Smith took 3,500 men down the river on a pre-dawn amphibious raid to seize the Confederate garrison at Brown's Ferry and open a supply route to Chattanooga, which became known as the Cracker Line. The next day, along this route, Hooker's corps reached Chattanooga and further reinforcements from Grant's Army of the Tennessee led by Major General William T. Sherman were on their way.

By mid-November, when Sherman's corps arrived in the area, Grant's forces at Chattanooga numbered 70,000. Bragg's army, however, was not as strong as when he had arrived at Chattanooga. On November 4 he had dispatched Lieutenant General James Longstreet's corps from Chattanooga to Knoxville in east Tennessee, in an attempt to take the town from Major General Ambrose R. Burnside's Union Army of the Ohio garrisoned there. This reduced the number of men under his command at Chattanooga to 40,000, reorganized into two corps under Lieutenant General William J. Hardee and Major General John C. Breckinridge.

Grant planned to raise the siege by attacking the rebel line encircling the city on the landward side from Lookout Mountain in the southwest to Missionary Ridge, running from southeast to northeast of the city. Hooker's corps on Grant's right would make a diversionary attack at Lookout Mountain and likewise Thomas would hold the center at Chattanooga while Sherman's corps would launch the main attack on Bragg's right, at Tunnel Hill, rolling up the Confederate lines as he swept down Missionary Ridge. Rain delayed Sherman on Grant's intended day of attack, September 21, and instead Grant ordered Thomas to move forward from his trenches at Chattanooga to a hill called Orchard Knob, halfway between the opposing armies.

Federal camp by the Tennessee River.

Grant had heard a rumor that Bragg was intending to abandon the siege and Thomas' move was intended as a reconnaissance.

On November 23 Thomas' Army of the Cumberland brushed aside Confederate outposts to occupy Orchard Knob. Bragg, little more than a mile away on Missionary Ridge, saw the danger and pulled a division from Lookout Mountain on his left to strengthen his center. The next day Grant launched his attacks on Bragg's left and right wings. Sherman crossed the Tennessee north of Chattanooga but, having pushed aside light Confederate defenses across the river, stopped short of Tunnel Hill. Drawing up his forces on a nearby hill, he prepared for the attack on Missionary Ridge the following day. Meanwhile, at the other end of the line on November 24, Hooker had led his men across the river below Lookout Mountain and marched along the far bank to the mountain.

Facing Hooker's corps on Lookout Mountain was one Confederate division commanded by Major General Carter L. Stevenson. In thick mist, Hooker attacked the heavily outnumbered Confederates at 08:00. Stevenson was pushed back but managed to hold the Union troops on the steep slopes and the summit until the end of the day in what became known as the "Battle of the Clouds." At nightfall the Confederates retired from the mountain, before they were cut off from the rest of their army, and joined their comrades on Missionary Ridge.

Bragg still resolved to hold his three-mile-long front on Missionary Ridge, believing that the high ground gave him an advantage over Grant. Breckinridge's corps was to hold his right wing, and Hardee's corps his left, on the southern end of the ridge. At dawn on November 25 Sherman moved again, attacking the northernmost division on the ridge under the command of Major General Patrick R. Cleburne. Cleburne

Portrait of Maj. Gen. William F. Smith.

put up stubborn resistance on Tunnel Hill, and in spite of Sherman's overwhelming numbers the Union force hammered against him without success into the afternoon.

Grant's plan for the day had been for Thomas to occupy Bragg's well-defended center while the two flanking attacks led by Sherman and Hooker would turn and destroy the Confederates, but events overtook him. Fearing that Cleburne could actually turn his own left wing, at 15:30 Grant ordered Thomas to advance to take Confederate rifle pits at the foot of Missionary Ridge. The 25,000-strong Army of the Cumberland swept forward from Orchard Knob and swept aside the Confederate line of defense at the rifle pits. Seeing that they had thrown the Confederate defenders into panicked retreat, the Union army spontaneously continued its advance up the ridge. Unable to stop the attack, Thomas' officers joined in the headlong scramble up the steep slopes. Reaching the crest they swept aside Bragg's divisions in the center, seizing Confederate artillery and turning it on the remaining defenders. Hardee, now finding himself isolated on the Confederate left, held on until nightfall then retreated with Cleburne's still defiant division under the cover of dark, to follow the shattered remnants of Bragg's army toward Georgia.

Sketch of Chattanooga, Tenn., and the military positions.

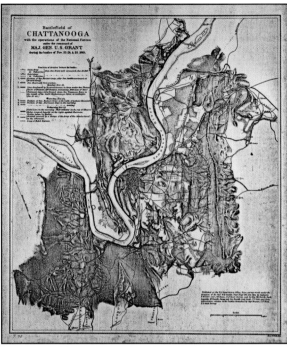

Map of the battlefield of Chattanooga showing Grant's operations.

PARTICIPATING UNITS:

Confederates: ....General Braxton Bragg, Army of Tennessee, 40,000

Union: ....Major General Ulysses S. Grant, Army of the Cumberland (Major General George H. Thomas) and Army of the Tennessee (Major General William T. Sherman) combined total 70,000

THE BATTLE:

Duration of battle: ....Three days; September 23–25, 1863

Location of battle: .....Chattanooga, Tennessee

Outcome: ....Union victory

CASUALTY FIGURES:

Confederates: 6,700

Union: 5,800

View of the battlefield of Cold Harbor, Va.

BATTLE OF THE WILDERNESS MAY 5, 1864

In the aftermath of the titanic struggle of the Battle of Gettysburg, both sides took time to recover, but by the start of the new year, the Union was ready to make a new move in the war in the east. In March 1864, the victor of many battles in the west, Major General Ulysses S. Grant, was called to Washington to be promoted to Lieutenant General and made commander-in-chief of all Union forces in the field. It was hoped he would transform the moribund war in the east against the Confederate General Robert E. Lee.

Grant planned a direct attack on Lee's Army of Northern Virginia, using Major General George G. Meade's Army of the Potomac, which would be coordinated with advances by Major Generals Franz Sigel along the Shenandoah Valley and Benjamin F. Butler on the Yorktown Peninsula to divert Lee's attention. Grant would travel with Meade but Meade would nominally retain command of the army, which had been encamped on the northern bank of the Rapidan River in Virginia since Meade's unsuccessful foray south towards Lee's army in November the previous year.

On May 4 the Army of the Potomac crossed the Rapidan and headed towards the heavily wooded area known as the Wilderness, where the Battle of Chancellorsville had been fought the previous year. Lee planned to attack Grant in the Wilderness, hoping to take advantage of the difficulties of visibility and movement in the dense bush and nullify the disparity in numbers—Grant/Meade's army numbered 100,000 while Lee had only 60,000 men.

Grant knew the dangers posed by the Wilderness but resolved to move quickly, hoping to steal a march on Lee and be through the Wilderness

Burial of soldiers after the fighting at Fredericksburg, Va.

before Lee had time to react but once in the thick woods he was marching blind, something compounded by his lack of cavalry scouts. Lee, on the other hand, had deployed his cavalry in reconnaissance and, once he received news that Grant had crossed the river, anticipated Grant's movements along two of the few roads through the Wilderness and set off in pursuit.

At dawn on May 5 Lee's advance corps, led by Lieutenant General Richard S. Ewell followed by Lieutenant General Ambrose P. Hill, encountered the column of Union infantry along the Orange Turnpike, near the Wilderness Tavern. Major General Gouverneur K. Warren's corps counterattacked and the fighting soon became a melee, the gunsmoke in the impenetrable underbrush reducing visibility still further. Grant ordered Major General John Sedgwick's corps to enter the line on the Union's right flank, while Major General Winfield S. Hancock's corps was to support Warren on the right, taking Hill on the Orange Plank Road. The fighting intensified as Lee and Grant threw more reinforcements into the battle and patches of woodland were set alight, many wounded burning to death. Grant's attempt to mount a full-scale counterattack became impossible in the chaos, Hancock only advancing at 16:00. The fighting continued until nightfall, when the two armies established their positions along the five-mile front.

During the night Grant resolved to attempt another full-scale assault and arranged his army accordingly. Sedgwick and Warren would continue to hold Ewell on the right and Hancock would renew his assault on Hill's position on the left flank while Major General Ambrose E. Burnside's corps, which had arrived that evening, would break through the weakened center.

Pontoon bridge over the James River, Va.

At 05:00 Hancock struck Hill's positions, overwhelming the Confederate lines within the hour. Fortunately for the Confederates, Lieutenant General James Longstreet's corps arrived along the Orange Plank Road at that moment and drove into Hill's men. By 08:00 the Union troops were now being driven back on the left wing, and to make matters worse, Burnside had failed to capitalize on Hancock's earlier success, mounting only a delayed, desultory attack.

Lee, sensing the battle was turning his way, reinforced Longstreet's wing and Longstreet renewed his assault in late morning, this time turning Hancock's exposed flank. In the fighting Longstreet was seriously wounded by his own troops and as Hancock withdrew his men, the attack ground to a halt.

Lee attempted two further attacks in the center and on his left wing at 14:00 and 16:30, but by then Burnside's corps was fully in the field and the attacks were broken up. Although Brigadier General John B. Gordon's division threatened to turn Sedgwick's right flank at the end of the day, the battle died out as night fell. Both sides had suffered heavy casualties in the battle but neither side retreated. The next day Grant continued his march south through the Wilderness towards Spotsylvania Courthouse, the site of the next battle between the two armies.

Canvas pontoon bridge across the North Anna at Jericho Mills, Va.. Constructed by the 50th New York Engineers, the Vth Corps under Gen. Gouverneur K. Warren crossed here on the 23rd. View from the north bank.

This council of war at Massaponax Church, Va., includes Gen. Ulysses S. Grant, Gen. George G. Meade, Assistant Secretary of War Charles A. Dana, and numerous staff officers.

PARTICIPATING UNITS:
Confederates: ....General Robert E. Lee, Army of Northern Virginia, 60,000
Union: ....Lieutenant General Ulysses S. Grant, Army of the Potomac (Major General George G. Meade), 100,000, IX Corps, Army of the Ohio (Major General Ambrose E. Burnside), 20,000, total 120,000 men

THE BATTLE:
Duration of battle:....Two days; May 5–6, 1864
Location of battle:.....The Wilderness, Virginia
Outcome: ....Stalemate

CASUALTY FIGURES:
Confederates: 8,700
Union: 17,600

Body of a Confederate soldier near Spotsylvania Courthouse, Va.

BATTLE OF SPOTSYLVANIA MAY 8–19, 1864

Despite the heavy losses endured by the Union Army of the Potomac at the Battle of the Wilderness, May 5–6, 1864, Lieutenant General Ulysses S. Grant continued his advance into Confederate Virginia, determined to win the war of attrition against General Robert E. Lee's Army of Northern Virginia. Grant was aiming for the crossroads at Spotsylvania Courthouse, and on the evening of May 7 his first troops, Major General Gouverneur's Warren's corps, started to leave the defensive lines occupied since the battle the day before to head south through the Wilderness. Screened by Major General Winfield S. Hancock's corps, the remainder of Grant's army followed, and by the early hours of the morning, the leading Union troops had left the Wilderness and reached open ground.

Lee had to reorganize his army after the Battle of the Wilderness. Lieutenant General James Longstreet's wounds meant that his corps was given to Major General Richard H. Anderson, and then Lieutenant General Ambrose P. Hill was taken ill suddenly, necessitating his replacement as corps commander by Major General Jubal A. Early. Realizing that Grant's forces had slipped away, and that Grant was attempting to reach open ground and cut him off from Richmond, Lee dispatched first Anderson's then Early's corps in pursuit, as well as his cavalry. The Confederates won the race to reach the crossroads, just. Major General James E. B. Stuart's Confederate cavalry barely had time to erect their breastworks early in the morning on Laurel Hill when Warren's infantry arrived at about 08:00 on May 8. The hard-pressed cavalry had to send word to Anderson to bring reinforcements quickly and a rapid march brought the Confederate infantry to the battlefield shortly afterward to shore up the line.

The soldier's body is prepared for burial. It was from this direction that Ewell's Corps attacked the Federal right on May 19, 1864.

Despite their exhaustion from the overnight march, the Union force launched repeated attacks on the Confederate lines, and as further elements of both armies arrived in the area, the battle spread, although Hancock kept his corps by the edge of the Wilderness at Todd's Tavern, attempting to block Early's route. However, Early's men had taken a different path through the Wilderness and were able to reinforce the men on Laurel Hill. When Lee arrived at the battlefield in the early afternoon he could see that the Confederates held a strong position and were able to hold off the Union troops. Grant called off the attack later that day but still intended to make his advantage in numbers count, having 90,000 men as opposed to Lee's 50,000, and to continue his assault on the Confederates in the coming days, writing to President Lincoln, "I propose to fight it out on this line if it takes all summer."

The battle, in fact, lasted nearly two weeks. The day after the first encounter, both sides dug in, the Confederates' now formidably fortified defensive line forming a salient nicknamed the "Mule Shoe," before the Union troops continued their attacks on the 10th. Prompted by a brigade commander, Colonel Emory Upton, the Union force adopted a new formation of attack in columns rather than a line of infantry, to concentrate their fire. Using this tactic temporarily managed to break through the defenses of the Mule Shoe before lack of reinforcements forced their withdrawal.

Grant then planned a massive assault on the Mule Shoe, and on May 12 threw 60,000 men against the Confederate salient. Hancock's corps smashed through the Confederate defenses, but was driven out of that section of the salient, known as the "Bloody Angle," after a counterattack by the Confederate reserve corps led by Major General John B. Gordon and fierce hand-to hand fighting. The other Union attacks by Burnside's

View of Massaponax Church, Va., temporary headquarters of Gen. Ulysses S. Grant, surrounded by soldiers

and Warren's corps were more easily repelled, although fighting carried on along the line until midnight, and the Confederates managed to create another strong defensive line. The day's fighting had cost both sides dear—the Confederates suffered 5,000 casualties while the Union lost 6,800 in the attack—but Grant intended to fight on.

Although heavy rain prevented further major assaults on the Confederate lines for the next four days, Grant probed the flanks of the salient before renewing his frontal attack with Hancock's corps on the 18th. Still unsuccessful, he finally decided that Lee's position was too strong for a direct assault and, after holding a counterattack by Ewell's corps on his right on May 19, on May 20 Grant ordered first Hancock then the remainder of his army to move south out of the area around Spotsylvania Courthouse to continue his effort to outflank Lee's army. At the same time Lee also moved south to avoid being cut off from Richmond and the two armies would meet again within days at the North Anna River.

Ruins of the Richmond and York River Railroad bridge across the Pamunkey, above White House landing.

The Rappahannock River front during the evacuation of Port Royal, Va.

PARTICIPATING UNITS:
Confederates: ....General Robert E. Lee, Army of Northern Virginia, 50,000
Union: ....Lieutenant General Ulysses S. Grant, Army of the Potomac, 90,000

THE BATTLE:
Duration of battle: ....12 days; May 8–19, 1864
Location of battle: .....Spotsylvania Courthouse, Virginia
Outcome: ....Stalemate

CASUALTY FIGURES:
Confederates: 9–10,000
Union: 17,500

Portrait of Maj. Gen. Benjamin F. Butler.

BATTLE OF COLD HARBOR MAY 31–JUNE 12, 1864

Although Lieutenant General Ulysses S. Grant had eventually admitted defeat at the protracted Battle of Spotsylvania, he continued to move the Army of the Potomac south further into Virginia in his campaign of attrition against General Robert E. Lee's Army of Northern Virginia. His aim was to outflank Lee, cutting him off from the Confederate capital, Richmond, then destroy the Confederate army in open battle, maximizing his advantage in numbers (110,000 compared to 60,000). Lee managed to inflict further losses on Grant's forces as they attempted to cross the North Anna River on May 23, but was unable to make his advantageous position count and Grant was able to sidestep Lee again.

In his effort to block Grant's advance, Lee was being driven back towards Richmond. After the inconclusive skirmish at Totopotomy on May 30, Grant attempted yet again to outflank Lee, aiming for the vital road junction at Old Cold Harbor, sending his cavalry ahead under Major General Philip H. Sheridan. Lee had anticipated the move and had dispatched his own cavalry under his nephew Major General Fitzhugh Lee to the crossroads.

The two cavalry forces met at Old Cold Harbor on May 31, the Confederates being driven back from their defenses, but Confederate infantry reinforcements forced Sheridan to withdraw. There followed two days of skirmishing as both sides attempted to seize control of the crossroads and by June 2 Lee and Grant had dug in on their respective lines, seven miles long. The Confederates established a line of trenches with Major General Jubal A. Early's corps on the left flank in the north, Major General Richard H. Anderson's corps in the center, and Lieutenant General Ambrose P. Hill's corps on the right flank in the south. They

Generals of the Army of the Potomac: Gouverneur K. Warren, William H. French, George G. Meade, Henry J. Hunt, Andrew A. Humphreys, and George Sykes seen at Culpeper, Va.

were in a strong position but Grant was reluctant to continue his attempt to outflank Lee because he was nearing the swampy ground of the Chickahominy River on his left flank. Instead he resolved to make a huge frontal attack.

Grant launched his attack at daybreak on June 3, along a two-mile front. It was a massive charge of 60,000 men from three corps, led by Major Generals Winfield S. Hancock, Horatio G. Wright, and Major General William F. Smith, but the Confederates had prepared interlocking fields of fire and the Union infantry was slaughtered. Within a few minutes the Union lost 7–8,000 men and Grant was forced to abandon the attack. Although skirmishing continued at Cold Harbor for some days afterward, Grant realized he was unable to break through Lee's army. He would have to continue his flanking attacks, this time moving south of Richmond towards Petersburg.

PARTICIPATING UNITS:

Confederates: .... General Robert E. Lee, Army of Northern Virginia, 60,000
Union: .... Lieutenant General Ulysses S. Grant, Army of the Potomac, 110,000

THE BATTLE:

Duration of battle: .... 13 days; May 31–June 12, 1864
Location of battle: ..... Cold Harbor, Virginia
Outcome: .... Confederate victory

CASUALTY FIGURES:

Confederates: 1,500
Union: 7–8,000

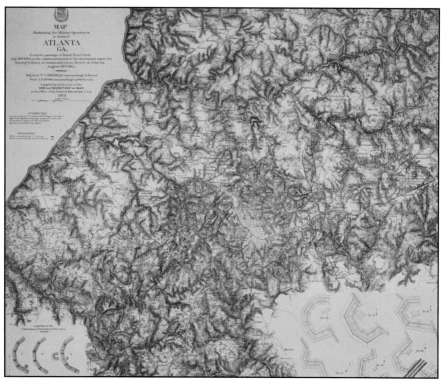

Map showing the siege of Atlanta.

ROUTE TO ATLANTA MAY–JULY 1864

When Lieutenant General Ulysses S. Grant was made commander-in-chief of all Union forces in the field in March 1864, he appointed Major General William T. Sherman to take over his forces in the west. The aim was to continue the successful drive against the Confederacy, following the capture of Chattanooga in November 1863. Sherman's key strategic objective was the second most important city of the Confederacy: Atlanta, Georgia.

Sherman had a massive force of approximately 110,000 men under his command, comprising three armies: Major General George H. Thomas' Army of the Cumberland (60,000), Major General James B. McPherson's Army of Tennessee (30,000), and Major General John M. Schofield's Army of Ohio (17,000). Facing him was General Joseph E. Johnston's Army of Tennessee comprising just two corps under Lieutenant Generals William J. Hardee and John B. Hood plus a cavalry division under Major General Joseph Wheeler. Although the Confederates only numbered 45,000, they were in a strong defensive position, occupying Rocky Face Ridge, near Dalton, commanding the surrounding mountainous terrain and deep river valleys that Sherman would have to traverse to reach Atlanta.

Sherman started to move his troops south of Chattanooga on May 4. He intended to hold Johnston at Rocky Face Ridge with Thomas' army while McPherson marched round the Confederates' flank to Resaca, cutting Johnston's supply lines at the railroad and forcing him to pull back toward Atlanta. However, when McPherson arrived at Resaca on

Gen. William T. Sherman, leaning on gun breach, at Federal Fort No. 7, Atlanta, Ga.

May 9 he discovered a larger than expected Confederate force holding the town and withdrew to Snake Creek Gap. Receiving news of this Union army to his rear Johnston decided to withdraw the rest of his army to Resaca on May 12, to await the arrival of reinforcements in the shape of Lieutenant General Leonidas Polk's corps which would bring his total forces to 60,000.

Sherman attacked Resaca over the next three days (May 13–15) and although the battle was inconclusive, Johnston decided to withdraw further south to Adairsville. There Sherman attempted to outflank the Confederate defenses, and Johnston pulled back again toward Cassville, where Johnston missed the chance to attack Schofield's Army of the Ohio which had become isolated in the area. Deciding that Johnston's defenses at Cassville were too strong, Sherman again attempted to outflank Johnston, and when Johnston reacted, the two sides met at the village of Dallas, Georgia on May 25.

A sequence of inconclusive battles ensued in the area over four days at New Hope Church, Pumpkin Vine Creek, and Pickett's Mills before Sherman again attempted to move round Johnston's left flank. He was blocked at Kennesaw Mountain, near Marietta, on June 27. This time Sherman attempted a frontal assault on Confederate lines but lost 2–3,000 in the battle compared to Confederate casualties of 500. Following this setback Sherman now moved round Johnston's right flank, who was forced to pull back first across the Chattahoochee River, then into the Atlanta fortifications themselves in early July. Johnston was removed from his command on July 17 by President Davis in response to what he regarded as his excessive caution.

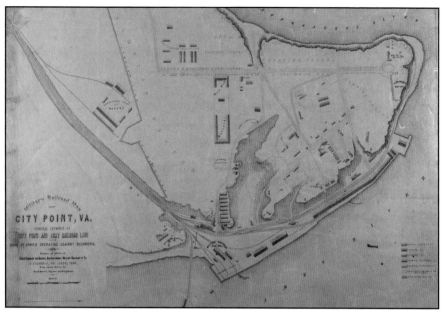

Map of City Point, Virginia, where Grant readied troops to go to Washington's aid.

BATTLE OF THE MONOCACY JULY 9, 1864

Known as the "Battle that Saved Washington," the engagement at Monocacy River, in Frederick County, was fought between the Union forces under Major General Lew Wallace and the Confederates under Lieutenant General Jubal A. Early on July 9, 1864.

After marching north through the Shenandoah Valley from Lynchburg, Early's army avoided the Union garrison at Harpers Ferry by crossing the Potomac River at Shepherdstown and thus entered Maryland. To prevent his advance a makeshift Union force, led by Wallace, was supplemented by Rickett's Division of the 6th Corps from the Petersburg line. The initial phase of the battle saw Wallace's force outflanked by a Confederate division under Gordon and subsequently suffering a defeat after strong resistance. However, behind the Union lines, Grant, hearing of Early's incursion, had embarked the balance of the 6th Corps on transports at City Point for rapid movement to Washington in order to bolster the city's defense. While Wallace was defeated at Monocacy River, the delay caused to Early's advance was sufficient to allow these experienced troops to reach Washington before Early reached the outskirts of the city on July 11. During skirmishes the following day, a spectator wearing a stove-pipe hat was noticed by Captain Oliver Wendell Holmes, Jr of the 6th Corps. Holmes shouted out to the figure, "get down, you damn fool, before you get shot," without recognizing that the figure he was addressing was none other than Abraham Lincoln. History records the fact that Lincoln took the advice, otherwise the Confederate sharpshooters may well have put Booth out a job.

As far as the Confederate assault was concerned, the arrival of the 6th Corps to bolster the city's defense allied to the fact that further Union

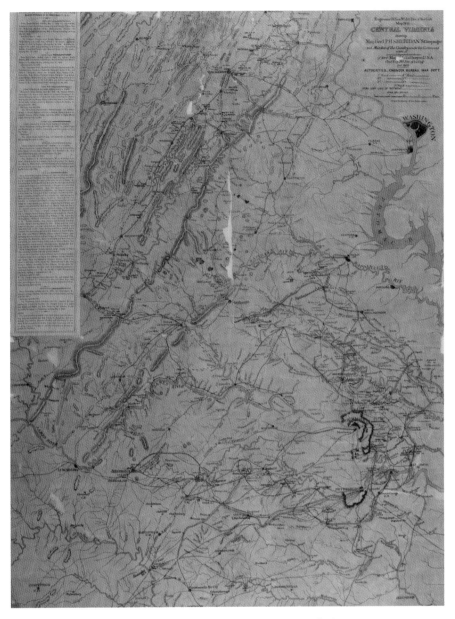

The routes of Sheridan's cavalry raids into Central Virginia, 1864–65.

soldiers were arriving to his rear, encouraged Early to make a strategic withdrawal back across the Potomac.

PARTICIPATING UNITS:

Confederates: .... Lieutenant General Jubal A. Early's Army of the Valley, 14,000

Union: .... Major General Lew Wallace, disparate force including 8th Illinois Cavalry and 3rd Division (Brigadier General James B. Ricketts), 6,000

THE BATTLE:

Duration of battle: .... Ten hours; July 9, 1864

Location of battle: ..... Frederick County, Maryland

Outcome: .... Confederate victory

CASUALTY FIGURES:

Confederates: 900

Union: 1,294

Portrait of Rear Adm. David G. Farragut.

BATTLE OF MOBILE BAY AUGUST 2–23, 1864

Although the Union had endeavored to maintain a strict blockade of most of the ports serving the Confederacy, there were a small number that had proved capable of blockade running. The last of these in the Gulf to the east of Texas was Mobile, and it was to this destination that the victor of New Orleans, David Farragut, was dispatched with a small fleet comprising 14 wooden ships and four monitors during the summer of 1864. Before approaching the port itself, Farragut had to neutralize the three ports that guarded the entrance.

On August 5, 1864, his flotilla approached the ports and a vicious firefight ensued. At one stage, in order to gain a better view of the conflict, Farragut clambered the mainmast of his flagship, the U.S.S. Hartford, onto which he was lashed by the quartermaster. As part of their defenses, the Confederates had spread mines and one of these was to sink one of Farragut's quartet of monitors, drowning 90 men as the ship sank. Urging his fleet on, Farragut commented, "Damn the torpedoes! Full steam ahead."

Having breached the first line of the Confederate defenses, Farragut's fleet took on a Confederate flotilla led by the Confederate ironclad, the C.S.S. Tennessee. Although this vessel was powerful, it was also unwieldy and, ultimately, the Union forces proved victorious. Over the next three weeks, joint action by the Union navy and army captured the three forts and while Mobile itself remained in Confederate hands, the action had closed another of the blockade-breaking ports.

Portrait of Commodore Franklin Buchanan, C.S.N.

PARTICIPATING UNITS:

Confederates: ....Admiral Franklin Buchanan, three gunboats and an ironclad; land forces under Brigadier Richard L. Page

Union: ....Admiral D. Farragut, 14 wooden ships and four monitors; army units under Major General Gordon Granger

THE BATTLE:

Duration of battle: ....21 days; August 2–23, 1864

Location of battle: .....Mobile Bay, Alabama

Outcome: ....Union victory

CASUALTY FIGURES:

Union: 322

Confederates: 1,500

Federal soldiers by gun in captured fort, Atlanta, Ga.

BATTLES AROUND ATLANTA JULY 14–SEPTEMBER 2, 1864

Between May and July 1864, Union Major General William T. Sherman had advanced from Chattanooga almost to Atlanta, outmaneuvering General Joseph E. Johnston's Army of Tennessee until the Confederates were pushed back within the fortifications of the city. On July 17 President Davis, frustrated at Johnston's passivity, relieved him of his command and replaced him with one of his corps commanders, Lieutenant General John B. Hood.

Sherman's forces crossed the Chattahoochee River on July 14 to the north of Atlanta and by the 17th two of his armies—Major General George H. Thomas' Army of the Cumberland (60,000) and Major General John M. Schofield's Army of Ohio (17,000)—were converging only five miles away from the city. His third force, Major General James B. McPherson's Army of Tennessee (30,000), was established east of the city at Decatur. Atlanta prepared itself for the inevitable siege.

Faced with strangulation by a much larger army (Sherman had 100,000 under his command compared to Hood's 50,000), Hood decided to replace Johnston's strategy of caution with a more aggressive approach in an attempt to drive Sherman away from Atlanta. He had an opportunity while Sherman's armies were still separated, but Thomas' Army of the Cumberland had crossed Peachtree Creek on September 19, and by the time Hood attacked on the afternoon of the 20th the Union troops had time to establish a strong defensive position.

Hood attacked with two corps led by Lieutenant Generals Alexander P. Stewart and William J. Hardee—a total of 20,000 men—and initially threatened the Union lines. Thomas rallied his men and the Confederates were beaten back at dusk after two hours' fighting, the attackers losing

Gen. William T. Sherman on horseback at Federal Fort No. 7, Atlanta, Ga.

5,000 men in the battle.

In spite of his failure to turn back the Union army at Peachtree Creek, Hood decided next to attack McPherson's Army of Tennessee at Decatur. Hardee's corps was dispatched the next day, July 21, on a long march back to Atlanta then east to outflank McPherson and to attack him in the rear, while the remainder of Hood's forces pulled back behind prepared fortifications north of Atlanta. Hardee's men were in a position to attack early on July 22. Despite their exhaustion they drove into McPherson's flank midmorning. Again the Union troops were in well-prepared positions and although McPherson was killed in this Battle of Atlanta—shot refusing to surrender when he blundered into the Confederate lines—and the Unionists lost 3,700 men, the Confederates failed to break through and themselves lost 7,500 men.

Sherman then increased the pressure on Atlanta, cutting off its railroads and shelling the city. His next move was intended to take the city from the west. McPherson's replacement, Major General Oliver O. Howard, was ordered to march his men round the south of Atlanta while Thomas and Schofield's corps occupied Hood to the north. Hood, however, countered by sending Lieutenant General Stephen D. Lee's corps to hold the Union forces at the crossroads at Ezra Church, intending Stewart's corps to then enter the battle on the Union's left flank and defeat Howard. However, when Lee reached Ezra Church, Howard's men were already in position and in the ensuing Battle of Ezra Church on July 28 the attacking Confederates again suffered heavy losses, 5,000, compared with Union losses of 562.

In little over a week Hood had lost 17,500 men, reducing his overall army to less than 35,000, and he was forced to abandon his

Atlanta after it fell—the railroad depot and yard; Trout House and Masonic Hall in background

offensive strategy and withdraw into Atlanta's defensive fortifications. Sherman tightened his grip on the city in the next month, attempting to break the Confederates' hold on the last railroad route into the city, the Montgomery & Atlanta Railroad to Macon and Jonesboro, and advancing his siege works towards the Confederates' lines. At the end of the month a desperate Hood sent Hardee's and Lee's corps south towards Jonesboro in a final attempt to avoid being encircled and cut off. He hoped to outflank Sherman's forces which were inching towards the crucial rail junction at East Point but the Union forces were well entrenched and easily repulsed the Confederates' attack on August 31.

Hardee was left isolated at Jonesboro while Lee was pinned down outside Atlanta and Hood had no option then but to abandon the city if he was to save the remnants of his army. Hood ordered Lee to disengage and, loading as many supplies as he could on railway carriages before destroying the remainder, evacuated the city with his remaining forces on September 1. The Union troops could see the fire of Hood's destroyed supplies, the ammunition exploding into the night sky, and the next day, September 2, the triumphant Sherman entered Atlanta, sending a cable—"Atlanta is ours, and fairly won"—announcing his triumph. The victory at Atlanta was widely celebrated in many northern cities and it also helped to secure Sherman in his position as the Union's foremost commander, with many commentators comparing him favorably with the great military leaders, such as Napoleon, from the past.

Atlanta after it fell—soldiers on boxcars at railroad depot.

Atlanta after it fell—Trout House, Masonic Hall, and Federal encampment on Decatur Street

Atlanta after it fell—Confederate palisades, on north side of city.

New Market, Va., battlefield, May 15, 1864.

SHENANDOAH VALLEY CAMPAIGN APRIL–OCTOBER 1864

One of the coordinated elements of Lieutenant General Ulysses S. Grant's strategic plan when he was appointed commander of all Union forces in the field in March 1864 was an attack down the Shenandoah Valley in Confederate Virginia. The valley was a major food-producing area for the Confederacy and would be lightly defended while the Confederate General Robert E. Lee's Army of Northern Virginia was preoccupied with defending Richmond from Grant.

On April 29 Major General Franz Sigel's 8,000 men of the Army of Western Virginia headed south towards the Shenandoah Valley from Martinsburg, West Virginia. To defend the valley the Confederates could call on only Major General John C. Breckinridge's two brigades and a cavalry brigade led by Brigadier General John D. Imboden—in all, approximately 5,000 men.

Sigel was aiming for Staunton on the Virginia Central Railroad, but Breckinridge advanced north to meet him, pausing at Staunton on May 8, where he added a cadet corps from the nearby Virginia Military Institute to his force. By May 15 the two sides were converging on New Market, 40 miles north of Staunton. Breckinridge established defensive lines on high ground to the south of the town—Shirley's Hill—preparing for an attack by Sigel. He, however, would not be drawn and instead remained in his positions in the town and on Manor's Hill and Bushong's Hill to the north of the town. During the morning of the 15th Breckinridge went on the attack, pushing the Union troops out of the town back over Manor's Hill to Bushong's Hill. Imboden's cavalry attempted to move round the Union force's left flank and succeeded in driving back Sigel's cavalry, but in doing so became isolated from the main battle on Bushong's Hill.

City Point, Va., Members of Gen. Ulysses S. Grant's staff.

Sigel had arranged his infantry in two lines on Bushong's Hill, intending the first line to break the Confederates' momentum while the second would finish them off. The Confederates broke through the first line but were halted and then driven back by the second. Sigel, however, delayed his counterattack, allowing Breckinridge time to bring up his reserves, including the corps of cadets, to reform his lines. When the Union attack came Sigel committed only 1,500 of his men and the Confederate line repulsed the attack. As the Unionists retreated at 15:00, the Confederates left their positions to follow, driving the Union troops off Bushong's Hill.

Sigel decided to pull back from the area and, with the assistance of his artillery, managed an orderly retreat, crossing the Shenandoah River to safety. The Confederates lost 550 men in the Battle of New Market and the Union approximately 850. The battle left Grant's Valley Campaign strategy was in tatters, so much so that Breckinridge was able to send a detachment of 2,500 men to assist Lee's campaign against Grant.

On May 19 Sigel was replaced in command by Major General David Hunter, who in June advanced again into the Shenandoah Valley with 18,000 men. Following a campaign of destruction, Hunter was threatening the strategically important town of Lynchburg in mid-June and Lee was forced to detach 9,000 men under the command of Lieutenant General Jubal A. Early from his forces outside Richmond to defend the valley. If possible, Early was also to repeat "Stonewall" Jackson's campaign of 1862 and threaten Washington, forcing the Union to pull troops away from Richmond to defend the capital. By June 16 Hunter was besieging Lynchburg, but Early's troops linked up with Breckinridge's small force opposing Hunter and although the Confederates still numbered only 15,000, Hunter chose to retreat, pulling out of the Shenandoah Valley into West Virginia.

Early then marched north and at Winchester temporarily divided his forces, intending to outflank Sigel who was still in command of 5,000 men at Harpers Ferry. Sigel, however, withdrew to Maryland's Heights, and Early continued his advance with his reunited army, crossing the Potomac River into Maryland on July 4. At Sharpsburg Early split his forces again, sending a detachment to Hagerstown to exact a payment of $200,000 from the townsfolk as reparation for Hunter's campaign of destruction in the Shenandoah Valley, while Early headed towards Frederick to demand the same.

Early's advance now forced Grant to send first a division, then Major General Horatio G. Wright's corps, from the Army of the Potomac fighting Lee to reinforce the 2,000 men under Major General Lewis Wallace defending Washington. When Early's men left Frederick on July 9 they encountered Wallace's force, strengthened by the first 5,000 men from Grant's army, blocking his way by the Monocacy River (see page 162). In the ensuing battle on the 9th Wallace managed to hold Early at first, but by the end of the day the Union troops were overwhelmed, and retreated to Baltimore. Meanwhile Early continued his advance towards Washington, which he reached on July 10. Early probed the defenses of Fort Stevens, one of the ring of fortifications guarding Washington, and decided that the capital's defenses were too strong to attack and that he had achieved his campaign's objectives. That night Wright's corps launched an attack on Early's men at Fort Stevens, who conducted an orderly retreat from the outskirts of the city. By July 14 Early's army was back in Confederate Virginia.

Grant, however, resolved to put an end to the potential threat posed by Early's army, and in early August replaced Hunter as commander of the Union troops in the area with Major General Philip H. Sheridan. Sheridan had 43,000 men under his command compared to Early's 14,000. A cat-and-mouse campaign ensued. On August 21 Early launched an abortive attack on Sheridan's forces at Charles Town, West Virginia, before advancing northward to Harpers Ferry. Sheridan did not withdraw his forces across the Potomac, but instead dug in at Berryville and threatened Winchester. Early's army was then further weakened when he had to send a division to support Lee at Petersburg and on September 19 Sheridan attacked Early at Winchester, forcing the Confederates to retreat south of Strasburg with the loss of 4,000 men.

Sheridan attacked again on September 22, the Confederates losing 1,235 to Union losses of 528 on Fisher's Hill. This time Early withdrew to New Market, although his cavalry attempted a raid on Sheridan near Fisher's Hill on October 6 before being heavily defeated on October 9 at Tom's Brook. Sheridan followed Early, leaving a trail of destruction in his wake, until he drew up his forces across the valley at Cedar's Creek. Early decided that he could overrun Sheridan's position and attacked on the morning of October 19. The initial attack was successful but although the Confederates had taken most of the Union camp Sheridan, arriving

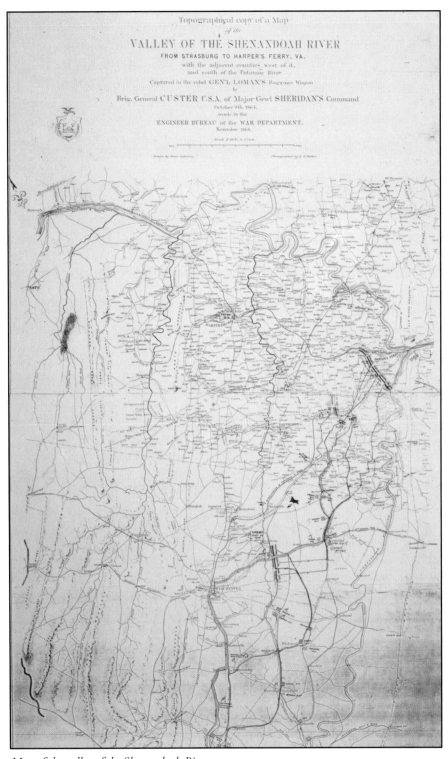

Map of the valley of the Shenandoah River.

by train from Washington later that day, regrouped his forces and drove the Confederates from the field. The Confederates lost 8,000 men in the battle, compared to Unionist casualties of 5,665, and Early's army had virtually ceased to exist. The Union was finally in control of the Shenandoah Valley.

Fort Abbott, City Point line, the fort occupied by Abraham Lincoln, in front of Petersburg, that resulted in its capture.

LINCOLN RE-ELECTED AUTUMN 1864

Despite the fact that the nation was at war, Lincoln faced re-election in the autumn of 1864. In the election, Lincoln again stood as a Republican—or Union as the Republican part called itself in 1864— but was faced by a new Democratic opponent in General McClellan, the erstwhile commander-in-chief of the Union army, who had been sidelined following his departure as commander in chief in late 1862.

There were a number of controversial issues that marked the campaign, most notably the concerns over prisoners of war and how best to achieve peace with the south. To the Republicans peace could only be achieved through victory; the Democrats, however, were widely considered to favor a less draconian settlement, including possibly peace through negotiation.

Undoubtedly, while not having a vote in the northern states' presidential election—for obvious reasons—the south favored the Democrats; indeed, reports from the front indicated that deserters from the Confederate forces commented that the Confederate army was fervent in its hope of a McClellan victory. While the Union army might have been considered likely to support its erstwhile commander, in reality the army—where individual states had given it the vote—voted four to one in favor of Lincoln, a higher percentage support than Lincoln achieved amongst the civilian population. In the election, Lincoln had a majority of half a million, securing the electoral college by 212 to 21. He won all of the states voting, with the exception of Kentucky, Delaware, and New Jersey.

Allan Pinkerton, President Lincoln, and Maj. Gen. John A. McClernand.

Federal outer line at Nashville, Tenn.

BATTLES OF FRANKLIN & NASHVILLE NOV 30 1864 & DEC 15-16 1864

After General John B. Hood pulled out of Atlanta on September 1, 1864, leaving the city to the Union under Major General William T. Sherman, he regrouped in Palmetto immediately south of the city before moving north at the end of the month with his Army of Tennessee, now 35,000 strong. He intended to disrupt Sherman's lines of communications, particularly along the railroads out of Atlanta, and draw him out of Atlanta into a campaign that the Confederates could win, forcing Sherman back into Tennessee.

In early October Hood started his campaign of disruption, cutting railroads north of Atlanta. Sherman decided to pursue him, leaving a token force in Atlanta and also dispatching Major General George H. Thomas with a division to defend the strategically important Tennessee city of Nashville in case Hood should march north. Although the two armies clashed on the 15th at Snake Creek Gap, Hood was able to withdraw further west to Gadsden, Alabama. At this point Sheridan decided that Hood was leading him a wild goose chase as he was being pulled further and further away from Atlanta, so he returned to the city to plan his own campaign—the "March to the Sea" through Georgia—leaving Thomas to hold Hood at his rear.

When he became aware that Sherman had split his forces, Hood revised his plans. He now, ambitiously, intended to take Nashville, defeating Thomas in the process, then march through Kentucky and continue eastward until he could join General Robert E. Lee and help to relieve the siege at Petersburg. However, Hood delayed his move into Tennessee, only crossing the Tennessee River into that state on November 21. By that time Sherman had decided that Thomas needed reinforcements and dispatched Major General David S. Stanley's IV

Fortified railroad bridge across Cumberland River, Nashville, Tenn.

Corps from the Army of the Cumberland, Major General John M. Schofield's XXIII Corps from the Army of the Ohio, and the three divisions of XVI Corps of the Army of Tennessee—a total of 60,000 men.

Schofield feared that Hood could isolate him, cutting him off from Nashville, so as Hood advanced he pulled back to Columbia, on the Duck River, on November 24. There the Union troops established a strong position, forcing the Confederates to cross the river further east. Once across, Hood again threatened to cut off Schofield. This time Hood missed his opportunity as the outnumbered Schofield managed to evade a planned attack at Spring Hill on the 29th and reach the comparative safety of Franklin's fortifications by dawn the next day.

On the afternoon of November 30 the pursuing Hood finally caught up with Schofield at Franklin. Although outnumbered by Hood's 40,000-strong force, the 26,000 Union troops had established strong defensive positions. At 15:30 Hood ordered a frontal assault with two of his corps led by Major Generals Benjamin F. Cheatham and Alexander P. Stewart. Although the Confederates overran two Union brigades on the flanks, Schofield's main defensive works held firm. The Confederates continued attacking in waves for five hours into the dark until Hood finally called off the attack, having lost 6,200 men, including six generals killed, to Schofield's losses of 2,326.

That night Schofield withdrew his forces from Franklin to continue his march to Nashville, reaching the safety of that city on December 1. There Thomas' other reinforcements had arrived, swelling the number of men under his command to 60,000.

Nashville Railroad yard and depot with locomotives; the capitol in distance.

When the pursuing Hood arrived outside the city the next day with his depleted Army of Tennessee, which now numbered only 23,000, he dug in along a line parallel to the Union defenses, hoping to tempt Thomas out to attack. Despite being urged by Grant to take the offensive immediately, Thomas waited over two weeks while the encamped Confederates endured freezing weather, completing his cavalry reconnaissance and organizing his troops in a V-shape in front of the city, on the bend of the Cumberland River, with Major General James B. Steedman's detachment on the far left, then Schofield's and Major General Thomas J. Wood's corps at the apex, with A. J. Smith's then Major General James H. Wilson's cavalry divisions on the right, before he decided to attack.

At 08:00 on December 15, as the fog rose, Thomas launched his attack out of the city. Steedman advanced against Cheatham's corps on Hood's right, but the Confederates had had time to build substantial earthworks and the attack was driven back. Thomas' main attack was to come on Hood's left. Wilson's cavalry and Smith's divisions moved round to attack Stewart's left flank at 10:00, followed at 12:30 by Wood's corps, the infantry attacks coordinated with Union artillery. As the Union troops rolled up the Confederate line from Stewart's positions toward Lieutenant General Stephen D. Lee's corps, Schofield joined the attack on the right flank with his reserve corps.

Hood realized he faced the collapse of his army and at dusk pulled back Schofield, Lee, and Cheatham from the battlefield. However, he chose not to retreat to safety but to hold new positions two miles south, with Cheatham and his cavalry now on his left, the remnants of Stewart's corps in the center, and Lee on his right. The next morning Thomas advanced again, his artillery bombarding Confederate positions before

Wood attacked Lee on the Confederate right. Hood reinforced his right but the attack on this flank was a diversion for Thomas' main attack which was led by Wilson and Schofield against Cheatham's line at 15:30, followed by Smith. As Wilson then Smith broke through the Confederate lines, Hood's left flank collapsed, and despite some valiant rearguard fighting Hood's entire army retreated in disorder. Hood had lost 5,500 men in the battle compared to Union casualties of 3,061 and the Battle of Nashville marked the end of the Confederate military threat in the West.

BATTLE OF FRANKLIN

PARTICIPATING UNITS:

Confederates: .... General John B. Hood, Army of Tennessee, 40,000
Union: .... Major General John M. Schofield, XXIII Corps, Army of the Ohio, 26,000

THE BATTLE:

Duration of battle: .... 5 hours; November 30, 1864
Location of battle: ..... Franklin, Tennessee
Outcome: .... Union victory

CASUALTY FIGURES:

Confederates: 6,200
Union: 2,326

BATTLE OF NASHVILLE

PARTICIPATING UNITS:

Confederates: .... General John B. Hood, Army of Tennessee, 23,000
Union: .... Major General George H. Thomas, IV Corps, Army of the Cumberland, XVI Corps, Army of the Tennessee and XXIII Corps, Army of the Ohio, total 60,000

THE BATTLE:

Duration of battle: .... 2 days; December 15–16, 1864
Location of battle: ..... Nashville, Tennessee
Outcome: .... Union victory

CASUALTY FIGURES:

Union: .... 3,061 casualties
Confederates: .... 5,500 casualties

Interior view of Fort McAllister, 14 miles south of Savannah; the Ogeechee River beyond.

SHERMAN'S MARCH TO THE SEA NOVEMBER–DECEMBER 1864

In October 1864 Major General William T. Sherman abandoned his pursuit of General John B. Hood's Confederate Army of Tennessee and returned to his base in Atlanta. There he intended to march east through Georgia to the Atlantic coast, to eliminate Georgia strategically from the Confederate war effort. His force of 62,000 men, divided into two wings under Major Generals Henry W. Slocum and Oliver O. Howard, left Atlanta in flames on November 15, having destroyed the city's railways, bridges, factories and public buildings.

The Confederates could muster only the state militia plus some disparate bands of cavalry to oppose Sherman and his army spread wide to follow his instructions to "forage liberally on the country." In effect, the two wings were to wreak wide parallel paths of destruction through Georgia, destroying railroads and pillaging the communities they passed through.

On November 22 the largest battle of the campaign took place, when the Georgia militia attacked a Union infantry rear-guard detachment from Howard's wing at Macon. The inexperienced Confederate troops suffered over 500 losses compared to Union casualties of 62, but they barely slowed Sherman's drive east. That day, the northernmost wing, led by Slocum, reached the state capital at Milledgeville, while Howard's wing took Macon further south.

The Confederates then resorted to desperate measures, pioneering the use of landmines, or "torpedoes," in an attempt to slow the marching Union troops: to no avail. By December 10 Sherman's two wings were converging on the outskirts of Savannah, on the coast. There the Confederates had gathered a force of 15,000 men under Lieutenant

Federal soldiers with big gun at Fort McAllister, Savannah.

General William J. Hardee to defend the city. The Confederates hoped that the city's formidable defenses and port open to supplies from elsewhere in the Confederacy would enable Hardee to hold Savannah.

Sherman's first move was to detach a division on December 13 to take Fort McAllister, 15 miles south of Savannah. U.S. Navy warships could now resupply his forces unmolested. Hardee, realizing he was about to be encircled in Savannah and that the city would not be able to withstand a siege, decided to evacuate. His men escaped across the Savannah River on the night of December 20, and Sherman entered the city the next day, wiring President Lincoln to present the city "as a Christmas gift."

Army engineers removing 8-inch Columbiad gun from Fort McAllister.

Crowd in front of Presidential reviewing stand, Washington, D.C.

CONGRESS APPROVES THE THIRTEENTH AMENDMENT JANUARY 1865

The Emancipation Proclamation could not end slavery permanently as it was only a wartime measure. To achieve the complete abolition of slavery, an amendment to the U.S. Constitution had to be enacted. There had been earlier efforts, most notably in 1861 when the House of Representatives passed an amendment, but it was not until three years after the failure of that year that progress towards the amendment gained momentum. On June 15, 1864, the House of Representatives voted 93–65 in favor; however, as a result of Democratic gains in the election of 1862, this was less than the two-third majority required, and so the amendment was lost despite having also passed in the Senate.

The election of 1864 saw many of these Democrats lose their seats, although they were entitled to remain in Congress until the new session started on March 4, 1865. With the Republicans now having a sufficient majority, Lincoln decided to call a special session to try for a bipartisan approach following on from a vote of January 31, 1865, when the old House voted 119–56 in favor of the amendment with some Democratic support and other absenting themselves. With the amendment now passed in Washington, it was up to the individual states to ratify it. By the end of March, 19 states had voted in favor and only three Union states, all of which had voted for McClellan in the 1864 presidential election (New Jersey, Kentucky, and Delaware), had not done so.

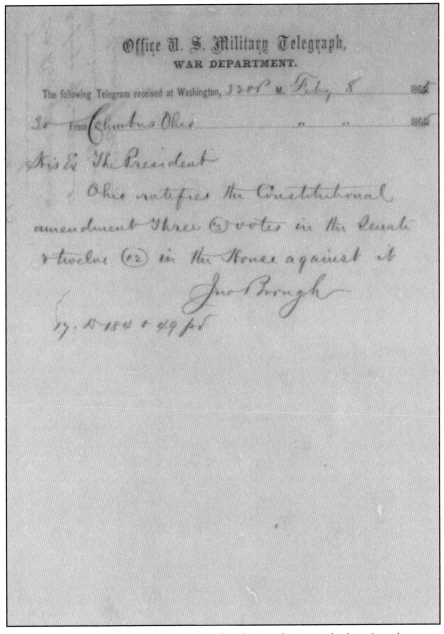

John Brough telegram reporting ratification of 13th Amendment to Abraham Lincoln, February 8, 1865.

The new amendment was formally ratified in December 1865 having been approved by 27 states (including eight from the south). There were two clauses to the Amendment:

1. Neither slavery nor involuntary servitude, except as punishment for crime whereof the party shall have been duly convicted, shall exist within the United States, or any place subject to their jurisdiction.

2. Congress shall have the power to enforce this article by appropriate legislation.

Fort Fisher, N.C.—the land front, showing destroyed gun carriage in second traverse.

FORT FISHER JANUARY 1865

By the late part of 1864, the only effective fighting force still available to the Confederate commanders was represented by Lee's Army of North Virginia and this was only able to function because it could be resupplied from the Carolinas via Fort Fisher at the mouth of the Cape Fear River. This made an assault on Fort Fisher an absolute necessity if the Union wanted to weaken Lee's force. The L-shaped fort—almost a mile long on the seaward side—was constructed with sand and dirt covered with marsh grass over a wooden frame. The walls were about 25ft in depth and rose to a height of between 10 and 30ft. The fort was defended by about 2,000 troops who had some 47 large guns to assist them.

To attack the fort, the Union assembled its largest naval task force of the war, comprising some 60 warships under the command of Admiral David D. Porter. There were also transports to ship the 6,500 soldiers under the command of Benjamin Butler. The first attempt to breach the fort occurred on December 24, 1864, when an elderly warship, loaded with 215 tons of gunpowder, was blown up close to the fort; this, however, proved a pointless exercise as did the efforts thereafter to shell the fort, since the barricades did their job well in absorbing the ordnance shot at them. A brief landing also proved inept as the assault troops discovered the strength of the defenders' guns and the fleet found that the approaches had been mined. The shambles represented by the first assault at Fort Fisher gave the Union commanders the long-desired opportunity to relieve Butler of his command, replacing him with a new commander, General Alfred Terry.

Interior view of the "Pulpit," Fort Fisher, N.C.

Interior view of Fort Fisher, showing traverse with dismounted gun.

Under Terry, a second assault was launched on January 15, 1865, when 4,500 soldiers attacked the fort from the north and a further 2,000 marines and sailors did the same from the sea. Although taking 1,000 killed and injured, the Union forces captured the fort, fundamentally weakening Lee's position inland.

Graveyard of the ruined Circular Church in Charleston, S.C.

CHARLESTON AND COLUMBIA TAKEN FEBRUARY 1865

During late 1864, the Union army under Sherman had cut a swathe through Georgia, culminating on December 21 with the capture of Savannah. Sherman's actions effectively ensured that Georgia's role in the Civil War had ended. He now turned his attention to South Carolina, heartland of the original rebellion. The Confederate authorities were aware of the threat that Sherman posed and on February 22, 1865, Joe Johnston was appointed commander of all Confederate forces in South Carolina in the hope that he would be able to prevent Sherman's forces from capturing the state. The reality was, however, that by this stage of the war, the forces available to the Confederate commander were strictly limited; the total manpower comprised some 20,000 soldiers, most of whom were drawn from already dispirited elements of the Confederate army—survivors of Hood's Army of Tennessee; the soldiers who had been evacuated from Savannah; the garrison of Charleston; and an element of cavalry recruited from South Carolina and sent back to defend their home state.

Against this less than impressive force Sherman had some 60,000 troops. Faced with these unfavorable odds, Johnston elected to divide his force in two, with half stationed at Charleston and half at Augusta, in the expectation that Sherman would initially attack one or other of these major cities. Sherman, however, had other plans: bisecting Johnston's army, he made straight for the state capital of Columbia.

Realizing that Charleston would be quickly cut off, Confederate forces withdrew from the city on February 18 and Union troops entered. The arriving troops, most of whom where from southern states of the Union, acted quickly to put out any fires caused by the retreating Confederates destroying munition stores. By this stage, however, Columbia had also

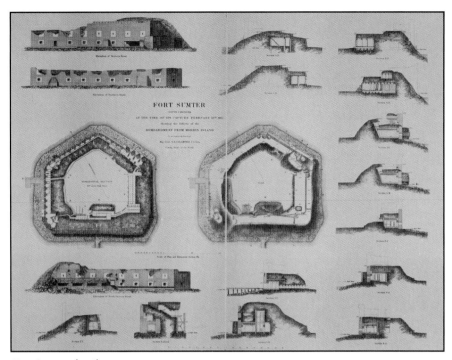

Fort Sumter details.

Ruins of the North Eastern Railroad depot, Charleston, S.C.

The fire-scarred Mills House; Hibernian Hall at left, Charleston, S.C.

fallen: units of Sherman's army occupied the town during February 17 and, by the following morning, half of Columbia had been reduced to rubble or ashes. The destruction of the city was a cause of much controversy, with Sherman blaming a high wind for fanning the flames from smoldering cotton bales left by the retreating Confederate forces. There were also accusations that many of Sherman's troops, well plied with alcohol, were themselves a cause of many of the fires; released Union prisoners, keen for revenge, were also blamed.

Undoubtedly, the Confederate authorities, too, can also take some of the blame in that they failed to deal with the burning cotton bales and also left the city replete with alcohol, which the locals used in the hope of bribing the arriving troops to remain peaceful.

Following his triumph in South Carolina, Sherman intended to head northward into North Carolina and thence to Virginia, where, if all went according to plan, he would meet up with Grant at Richmond. Events, however, were take over and the war was to be concluded before the Union's two great armies could meet up.

Crowd inside Fort Sumter.

View of ruined buildings through porch of the Circular Church (150 Meeting Street), Charleston, S.C.

Fort Fisher, interior view.

A CHANCE FOR PEACE LOST FEBRUARY 1865

Following the loss of Fort Fisher, Union control extended rapidly to most of the North Carolina coast. For Lee, the military position was worsening rapidly, as significant numbers of his army deserted (he lost 8 percent of his army through desertion in a single month).

To many in the south the loss of Fort Fisher represented one of the greatest disasters of the war and it led to increased stirrings of political opposition to Jefferson Davis and his administration. As a result of the pressure, Davis' Secretary of War, James A. Seddon, resigned and there was also pressure to replace Davis with Lee in a dictatorial role; in the event, Lee was appointed to the newly-created position of General-in-Chief. There were many, on both sides, who felt that the time was right for a negotiated peace. One of these was Francis Preston Blair, who put forward the proposal that the Union and Confederate forces should unite to attack the French in Mexico. While this scheme was never likely to proceed, Blair was given the opportunity to travel to Richmond, Virginia, to explore the possibilities of a negotiated settlement.

While both Davis and Lincoln were entrenched in their positions—the former refusing and the latter demanding unconditional surrender—both were willing to test the water. Davis established a commission of three—his Vice-President Alexander H. Stephens, Robert M. T. Hunter, and John A. Campbell—to meet Secretary of State William H. Seward at Hampton Roads. Although the initial prognoses were not positive, Lincoln himself joined the meeting, held on board the Union steamer River Queen, on February 3, 1865. However, Lincoln's unwillingness to abandon the policy of unconditional surrender, although willing to negotiate on other points, and the fact that the Confederate commission was not empowered to negotiate, ultimately doomed the talks to fail.

Interior view of Fort Fisher, with heavy gun broken by bombardment

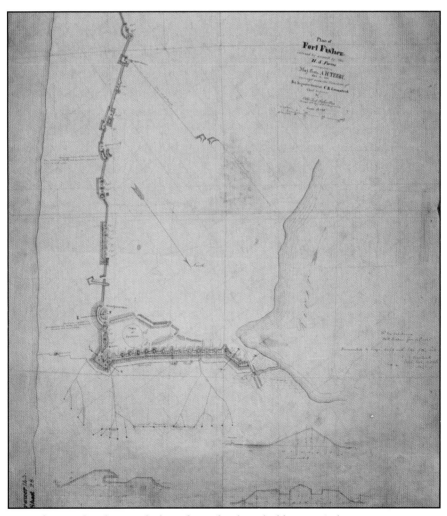

Map of Fort Fisher showing the line of torpedoes launched by Porter's ships.

The opportunity of an early peace was lost and Davis effectively ended the process by declaring to the Confederate Congress on February 6, 1865, that the fight must go on to avoid the "disgrace of surrender."

Barges on the canal; ruined buildings beyond, Richmond, Va.

BATTLE OF FIVE FORKS APRIL 1, 1865

The massive attack by Lieutenant General Ulysses S. Grant's Army of Potomac's on Confederate General Robert E. Lee's Army of Northern Virginia at Cold Harbor on June 3, 1864, had ended in failure, but Grant had managed to push Lee back into the defenses of Petersburg. Following a series of assaults on the formidable fortifications, Grant was forced to admit that the defenses were too strong to be taken by direct assault and he would have to settle down for a long siege, in which eventually his superiority in numbers would tell. In time both sides built vast systems of trenches and the battlefield came to resemble a scene from World War I.

Although stalemate descended on Petersburg, by spring 1865 the war elsewhere was obviously coming to a conclusion. The loss of the last Confederate seaport at Wilmington after Fort Fisher fell in January and the approach of Sherman's Union army through the Carolinas meant that the Confederacy was slowly being strangled. Although Lee's army was holding on in Petersburg, his supply lines were dwindling and the disparity between the size of his army (55,000) and Grant's, which had by this time grown to 125,000, was becoming insurmountable.

Lee decided he had to escape the war of attrition at Petersburg and attempt to join General Joseph E. Johnston's army defending the Carolinas against Sherman, if he was going to be able to prolong the war. First, he had to break out of the Union encirclement of Petersburg. In the early hours of March 25, 1865, Brigadier John B. Gordon's corps seized Fort Stedman on the Confederates' left for Lee, but Grant counterattacked and the Confederates were forced to abandon the fort

Crippled locomotive, Richmond & Petersburg Railroad depot.

later in the morning for the loss of approximately 4,000 men, compared to Unionist losses of 1,500.

Despite this setback, Lee realized that his extensive line of trenches running some 37 miles from Petersburg to Richmond was unsustainable. He intended to break out on his left, and reinforced his line in the west with Major General Fitzhugh Lee's cavalry and Major General George E. Pickett's infantry division. At the same time Grant also reinforced his line in the same area with Major General Philip H. Sheridan's cavalry, followed by infantry, probing the Confederate lines. On March 29 they encountered Confederates dug in at Dinwiddie Courthouse. The Union troops were halted in fighting which lasted two days, but Pickett, fearing he would be surrounded and destroyed by the advancing Union forces, withdrew towards Five Forks crossroads, on Lee's right on March 31.

During the morning of April 1 Pickett's men dug in at Five Forks, erecting barricades along a line in thickly wooded country 1.75 miles long, with cavalry posted at both flanks. Pickett had been instructed by Robert E. Lee to hold the vital crossroads "at all hazards" but that afternoon, believing they were safe from attack that day, both Pickett and Fitzhugh Lee left their troops to join Major General Thomas L. Rosser, whose reserve cavalry division was two miles to the rear, for dinner.

Fire Engine No. 3, Richmond, Va.

Park of captured guns at Rocketts, Richmond, Va.

Piles of solid shot, canister, etc., in the Arsenal grounds; Richmond & Petersburg Railroad bridge at right

They were wrong. Sheridan had ordered Major General Gouverneur K. Warren to bring his infantry corps into line at nearby Gravelly Run Church, then to advance at 16:30. At 17:00 Warren's 12,500 men struck Pickett's left flank.

The outnumbered Confederates at that part of the line could not stop the attack. Many fled or were captured as Pickett's left wing collapsed. The Union troops then attacked along the line and the Confederate right was first pushed back, then also fled the battlefield. It was only at this stage, when Pickett and Fitzhugh Lee saw the Union troops advancing toward them, that the Confederate commanders realized what was happening and rode toward the front line. Pickett attempted to rally his troops to attack the Union rear, to little avail, before retreating westward with the remainder of his force along a corridor held open by two of his brigades.

The Confederates had not only lost 2,950 men in the day's fighting but also Robert E. Lee's escape route to the west of Petersburg had been jeopardized. The next day, April 2, following an artillery barrage, Grant attacked along the length of the line and broke through again on the Confederate right at Poplar Springs. Lee realized that he could no longer hold on to his overstretched defenses in the face of such overwhelming numbers and that night began to evacuate Petersburg and Richmond, heading towards Appomattox.

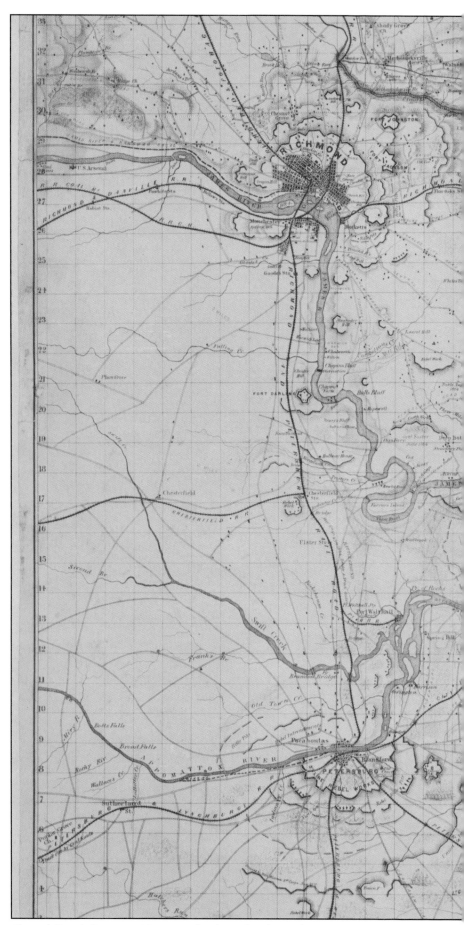

General Grant's Campaign War Map of Richmond and Petersburg

NOTE.

THE HORIZONTAL AND UPRIGHT LINES REPRESENT ONE MILE
SQUARE. BY REFERRING TO THE NUMBER ON THE LEFT AND TO
THE LETTER ON THE BASE, ANY POINT MAY BE FOUND TO SHOW
THE LOCALITY OF THE UNION ARMIES.
THUS, THE RANGE OF FIGURE 4 FOLLOWED UNTIL IT MEETS
THE RANGE OF LETTER L, SHOWS THE POSITION OF THE 5TH
ARMY CORPS ON THE WELDON R.R.
BY THIS METHOD THOSE IN THE ARMY ARE ENABLED TO
INFORM THEIR FRIENDS OF THE MOVEMENTS OF THEIR
COMPANIES AND THEIR LOCATION AND WILL ALSO SERVE AS
A JOURNAL TO EACH SOLDIER.

Pontoon bridges across the James, looking from Richmond toward Manchester.

Residence of Gen. Robert E. Lee, 707 East Franklin Street, Richmond.

Ruined buildings in the burned district of Richmond.

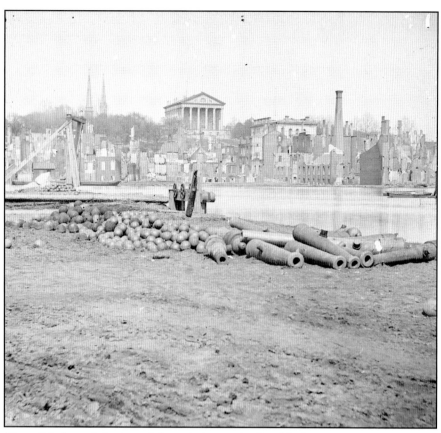

View of the burned district and the capitol across the Canal Basin.

View of James River and Kanawha Canal near the Haxall Flour Mills; ruins of the Gallego Mills beyond.

Ruins of Richmond & Petersburg Railroad bridge.

PARTICIPATING UNITS:

Confederates: ....Major General George E. Pickett, division of the Army of Northern Virginia, Major General Fitzhugh Lee, cavalry division of the Army of Northern Virginia, approx 15,000

Union: ....Major General Philip H. Sheridan, Sheridan's Command (Cavalry of the Armies of the James, the Potomac and the Shenandoah), 9,000; Major General Gouverneur K. Warren, V Corps, Army of the Potomac, 12,500, total 21,500

THE BATTLE:

Duration of battle:....One day; April 1, 1865
Location of battle:.....Five Forks, Virginia
Outcome: ....Union victory

CASUALTY FIGURES:

Confederates: 2,950
Union: 830

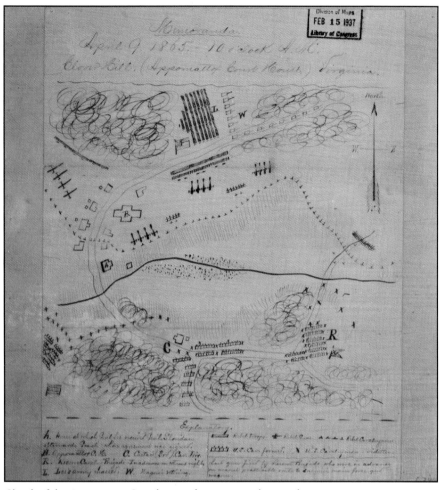

Sketch of the Appomattox Courthouse—by someone who was there.

APPOMATTOX COURTHOUSE APRIL 1865

By early 1865, the war was nearly over. Only three main areas—centered around North Carolina, along the coast east of New Orleans, and Texas—remained under Confederate control but these were cut off from each other as a result of the Union's military successes, in particular Sherman's march through Georgia and South Carolina. By April 1865, Lee's army had been reduced to some 35,000 men, a force which was brought together at Amelia Courthouse, some 35 miles from Richmond, with the intention of restocking. Unfortunately, in place of the anticipated (and much needed) food, the railway depot was filled with ordnance, which the army neither needed nor had the horses to move. In order to replenish his hungry force, Lee delayed his departure while food was sought. However, this delay was to have serious consequences, as it enabled Sheridan, with his cavalry and three infantry corps, on April 5 to cut off Lee's route southward to meet up with Johnston at Danville. Consequently, Lee was forced to turn west, towards Lynchburg, in the hope of further resupply. By this stage, Lee's army was on its last legs and, on April 6, some 6,000 of his weakened army was cut off by Sheridan's force at Sayler's Creek; for Lee the position was made all the worse by the fact that this loss included much of his ordnance. This situation was made all the more severe when on April 8, 1865, at Appomattox Station, a small force led Major-General George

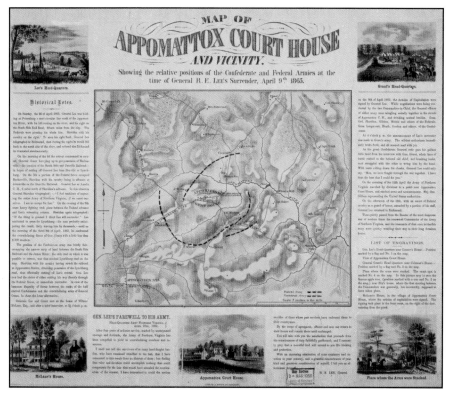

Map of the Appomattox Courthouse and vicinity produced some time after the event.

A. Custer—a commander later to achieve fame at the Battle of Little Big Horn during the Indian Wars—captured a supply train and 25 guns. This was a unique action in that it saw artillery unsupported by infantry fight against cavalry.

Lee's battered force headed towards Appomattox Courthouse where, on April 9, 1865, his forces initially managed to force the Union cavalry to retreat. However, the Union troops were quickly reinforced both from the front and rear making Lee's position unsustainable. Aware of the Confederate weakness, General Grant offered Lee the opportunity to surrender and Lee responded by asking for terms.

Initially, it seemed as though Lee would reject the terms, with several of his commanders suggesting that the Confederate force melt away and become a guerrilla force. Lee, however, rejected this option and offered his surrender. The terms agreed by Grant were remarkably generous and were accepted. Grant demonstrated compassion toward the beaten Confederate force by sending three days' worth of food to Lee's soldiers. The beaten Confederates officially surrendered their arms on April 12, 1865, bringing the war in Virginia to a close. In Washington, news of the surrender of Lee's army was marked by a 500-gun salute (for the earlier capture of Richmond, a 900-gun salute had been fired).

Fairfax Courthouse—house used as a headquarters by Gen. G. B. McClellan and Gen. P. G. T. Beauregard

FINAL SURRENDER APRIL–MAY 1865

With the surrender of Lee at Appomattox, despite Davis' endeavors to maintain the Confederacy as a military force, defeat was inevitable. Although Joseph Johnston's army was still active in North Carolina, the war was effectively over. In the following days the President of the Confederacy, Jefferson F. Davis, having evacuated Richmond, met with his cabinet and his remaining senior officers in the field, Generals Joseph Johnston and Pierre G. T. Beauregard, at Greensborough, North Carolina, to discuss the situation. Although Davis wanted to continue the fight, the generals and the majority of his cabinet wanted to sue for peace and on April 12, Davis conceded that Johnston could meet Major General William T. Sherman to discuss surrender terms.

In contravention of the orders that he had received, Joe Johnston surrendered with his army to Grant in the Carolinas on April 26, 1865. Other Confederate forces similarly surrendered. Davis, however, did not believe that the war was completely lost; he decided to head southward to Texas in order to regroup. In the event, however, he was captured at Ironsville, Georgia, on May 10, 1865, and was held, without trial, for two years at Fort Monroe, Virginia, being accused, among other crimes, of complicity in the assassination of Abraham Lincoln (a crime of which he was innocent). The final military actions of the Civil War took place far from the main theaters of war: small-scale engagements occurred in the North Pacific between pro-Union and pro-Confederate fishing boats until news of the final surrender of the south reached them.

Portrait of Gen. Joseph E. Johnston, Confederate Army.

The assassination of President Lincoln at Ford's Theater, Washington, D.C.

LINCOLN ASSASSINATED APRIL 14, 1865

When Abraham Lincoln was re-elected President in late 1864 the war was clearly beginning to turn in the favor of the Union. Victory had been achieved by the combatant with superior resources. Lincoln and his senior commander in the field, Lieutenant General Grant, had been the main proponents of a war of attrition estimated to have cost more than a million casualties. Moreover, many in the South felt that they were fighting for an independent way of life and that deeply cherished beliefs were being overrun. One such Confederate supporter was John Wilkes Booth, a well-known Maryland actor. Although eventually siding with the Union, Maryland had split loyalties and had a tradition of slave-owning. Before the war Booth had been a supporter of political groups dedicated to maintaining the slave-based economy of the Southern states and preserving the privileged status of white citizens. Lincoln's Emancipation Proclamation, issued on September 22, 1862, and effective from January 1, 1863, in which all slaves in rebel territories were to be freed, confirmed to these Southern sympathizers that a Union victory would result in the abolition of slavery throughout the United Sates.

During late 1864 Booth began to recruit like-minded individuals to form an underground group, dedicated to furthering the Southern cause. They are believed to have had some contact with the Confederate Secret Service, the intelligence agency of the Signal Corps, and hatched a plot to kidnap Lincoln and spirit him to the South, demanding independence for the Confederate States, or at least release of all the Confederate prisoners of war. The plotters planned to seize Lincoln on March 17, 1865, as he traveled in his carriage to visit Campbell Hospital outside Washington, but a last-minute change of plan by the President thwarted the would-be kidnappers. Before they had time to set up another

SURRAT.   BOOTH.   HAROLD.

War Department, Washington, April 20, 1865,

 # $100,000 REWARD!

THE MURDERER

Of our late beloved President, Abraham Lincoln,

IS STILL AT LARGE.

$50,000 REWARD

Will be paid by this Department for his apprehension, in addition to any reward offered by Municipal Authorities or State Executives.

$25,000 REWARD

Will be paid for the apprehension of JOHN H. SURRATT, one of Booth's Accomplices.

$25,000 REWARD

Will be paid for the apprehension of David C. Harold, another of Booth's accomplices.

LIBERAL REWARDS will be paid for any information that shall conduce to the arrest of either of the above-named criminals, or their accomplices.

All persons harboring or secreting the said persons, or either of them, or aiding or assisting their concealment or escape, will be treated as accomplices in the murder of the President and the attempted assassination of the Secretary of State, and shall be subject to trial before a Military Commission and the punishment of DEATH.

Let the stain of innocent blood be removed from the land by the arrest and punishment of the murderers.

All good citizens are exhorted to aid public justice on this occasion. Every man should consider his own conscience charged with this solemn duty, and rest neither night nor day until it be accomplished.

EDWIN M. STANTON, Secretary of War.

DESCRIPTIONS.—BOOTH is Five Feet 7 or 8 inches high, slender build, high forehead, black hair, black eyes, and wears a heavy black moustache.

JOHN H. SURRAT is about 5 feet, 9 inches. Hair rather thin and dark; eyes rather light; no beard. Would weigh 145 or 150 pounds. Complexion rather pale and clear, with color in his cheeks. Wore light clothes of fine quality. Shoulders square; cheek bones rather prominent; chin narrow; ears projecting at the top; forehead rather low and square, but broad. Parts his hair on the right side; neck rather long. His lips are firmly set. A slim man.

DAVID C. HAROLD is five feet six inches high, hair dark, eyes dark, eyebrows rather heavy, full face, nose short, hand short and fleshy, feet small, instep high, round bodied, naturally quick and active, slightly closes his eyes when looking at a person.

NOTICE.—In addition to the above, State and other authorities have offered rewards amounting to almost one hundred thousand dollars, making an aggregate of about TWO HUNDRED THOUSAND DOLLARS.

President Lincoln's box at Ford's Theater.

kidnapping, Lee surrendered his army at Appomattox Courthouse and the war was being concluded. Clearly, any demands for Southern independence had been overtaken by events.

The plotters met again to discuss their plans, and this time decided to assassinate Lincoln. Booth would murder the President; another of the group, Confederate agent George Atzerodt, would kill Vice President Andrew Johnson; and a third member, Lewis Paine, would kill Secretary of State William H. Seward. The murders would be carried out simultaneously and were intended to throw the Union into electoral chaos. Three of the plotters, including Booth, attended Lincoln's last public speech on April 11 in which he outlined his plans for the reconstruction of the Union after the war, including new rights for the slaves. The speech hardened the conspirators' resolve to assassinate Lincoln and derail the moves to end slavery.

During the closing days of the war Lincoln remained in Washington. At breakfast in the White House on Good Friday, April 14, his wife Mary Todd mentioned she would like to see the play Our American Cousin at Ford's Theater. After breakfast Lincoln returned to his office in the White House, seeing a number of visitors. He also sent a messenger to Ford's Theater to reserve the State Box for that evening. Later that morning, at 11:00, Lincoln chaired a cabinet meeting, also attended by

Rocking chair used by President Lincoln in Ford's Theater.

General Grant, at which the main topic of discussion was the postwar reconciliation between North and South and the plan of reconstruction for the South. The meeting continued to 14:00, and at the end of the afternoon, after further meetings, Lincoln broke off from his day's official work to join his wife in a carriage ride to Washington Navy Yard.

On their return the President and his wife dined at 18:00 and concluded his day's meetings before they set off for Ford's Theater just after 20:00. The Lincolns had originally hoped to attend the play with the Grants and the Stantons (Edwin M. Stanton was Secretary of War) but both sets of couples had declined their invitations and instead the President's carriage collected a young couple, Clara Harris and Major Henry Rathbone, en route. They arrived at Ford's Theater, on Tenth Street, at 20:30 and the party was shown to its seats. The play had already begun and there was a brief interruption while the house orchestra played "Hail to the Chief," and the audience rose to their feet before the evening's entertainment was resumed.

An hour later there were just the four members of the President's party in the box—the President's regular bodyguard, William H. Crook, had been unavailable for the evening and his relief, John F. Parker, had left the theater at the interval for a drink at a nearby bar and had not yet returned. At 10:15 Booth seized his opportunity. He entered a small

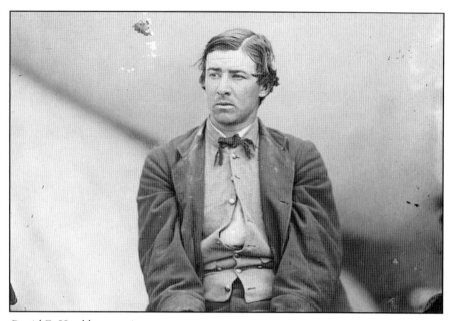

David E. Herold, a conspirator.

room behind the box then stepped out and fired a single pistol shot into the back of the President's head at point-blank range. Rathbone attempted to stop Booth but Booth slashed at him with his Bowie knife then leapt onto the stage, according to many accounts shouting, "Freedom" or "Sic Semper Tyrannis" (as always to tyrants), the state motto of Virginia. He landed awkwardly after the 11ft fall and broke a bone in his leg, but Booth had chosen a moment when only one actor was on the stage and still managed to make his escape to the back of the theater, where an accomplice was holding a horse for him. From there he rode to the Maryland coast that night, where accomplices spirited him away southward.

Lincoln was mortally wounded and was carried across the road to a boarding house, Petersen House. A bedside vigil was conducted through the night, a stream of doctors and senior officials visiting the comatose President, before Lincoln drew his final breath at 07:22 the next morning, April 15. Secretary of War Stanton declared, "Now he belongs to the ages."

The coordinated assassinations planned by the conspirators, however, did not succeed. Although Secretary of State Seward was attacked in his bed as he was recovering from a serious accident and suffered serious injuries, being stabbed in the face and neck, he escaped death, and the third conspirator did not carry out his attack on Vice President Andrew Johnson, enabling Johnson to be sworn in as President at 10:00 on the 15th.

Most of the conspirators were soon rounded up, but Booth managed to evade immediate capture. His leg was set by a doctor, Samuel Mudd, who it is believed also had links with the Confederate Secret Service

Samuel Arnold, a conspirator.

A portrait of John Wilkes Booth.

and who later claimed he had not known who Booth was, before he continued towards the Southern states with another conspirator, assisted by other agents. Pursuing U.S. cavalry were tipped off on April 25 that Booth was hiding in a barn on a tobacco farm belonging to Richard H. Garrett in Virginia and surrounded the building. Booth refused to come out and when the cavalrymen set fire to the barn a shot was heard, although some accounts suggest he was shot by one of the troopers. Booth was found inside the barn mortally wounded and expired shortly after.

George A. Atzerodt, a conspirator.

Execution of the conspirators: scaffold ready for use and crowd in the yard, seen from the roof of the Arsenal.

The four condemned conspirators (Surratt, Payne, Herold, Atzerodt), with officers and others on the scaffold; guards on the wall.

Hanging hooded bodies of the four conspirators; crowd departing.

Following Lincoln's assassination by John Wilkes Booth on April 14, 1865, the president's body was laid initially in state at the White House, where many notable visitors—such as General Grant, who wept openly at the catafalque on April 19—came to pay their last respects. Following the period of lying in state, the president's body was returned to Springfield, Illinois, by train.

The train left Washington at 08:00 for Baltimore on April 21, 1865, and followed almost the same route that Lincoln had traveled in 1861 as President-elect with the exception of Pittsburgh and Cincinnati but with the addition of Chicago. The locomotive carried a photograph of Lincoln over the cow catcher and the train carried, in addition to some 300 mourners, the remains of Lincoln's son Willie, who had died at the White House aged 11 in 1862 and whose remains were to be reinterred with his father's at Springfield. Also present was Lincoln's son Robert, although the President's widow remained mourning in Washington and did not travel to Springfield for the funeral. The President's body was also accompanied by a guard of honor.

It is estimated that the train's journey was witnessed by some seven million men, women, and children who stood by the trackside as the train passed by. At various points along the route the coffin was removed from the train, as at Baltimore where it was borne to the Merchant's Exchange Building to allow local residents to pay their final respects. The coffin was open at all of these events so that mourners could actually see the President; as the journey progressed, the face became increasingly discolored causing distress to some of the mourners and requiring the judicious application of make-up by the time the body had reached Illinois. In Philadelphia the coffin was placed in the East Wing of Independence Hall, where the Declaration of Independence had been signed. After Philadelphia, the train headed to New York and onward, finally reaching Springfield, Illinois, on May 3. The funeral took place on May 4.

THE NATION MOURNS.
FUNERAL MARCH
TO THE MEMORY OF
Abraham Lincoln.
THE MARTYR PRESIDENT.
NEW YORK.
Published by HORACE WATERS 481 Broadway.

President Lincoln's funeral procession on Pennsylvania Avenue, Washington, D.C.

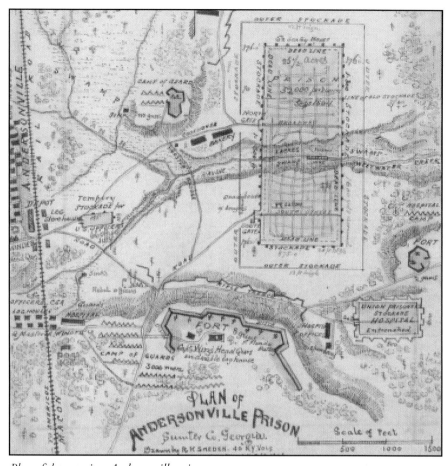

Plan of the notorious Andersonville prison.

ANDERSONVILLE MAY 1865

Andersonville, in Georgia, was the location of the most infamous of all the Confederate prison camps. As in all wars, the combatants captured large numbers of the opposing forces during the war, and both sides possessed camps that were inadequate and unhealthy. However, the death rate at Andersonville was notorious—albeit not the worst (that dubious honor went to Salisbury in South Carolina with a mortality rate of 34 percent as opposed to Andersonville's 29 percent)—and it was the single largest prison established by the south, housing no fewer than 33,000 in August 1864. Opened in February 1864, the camp was to have an active life of some 14 months before its closure, during which time some 12,000 prisoners died as a result of poor medical care, malnutrition, and contaminated drinking water. In addition, while the south had plentiful supplies of cotton and timber, it lacked the resources to convert these into decent accommodation for the prisoners, with the result that the detainees froze in winter and boiled during the summer. The camp's commander, Henry Witz, was tried in the U.S.'s first war-crimes trial and was executed by hanging on November 10, 1865. Witz was the only Confederate officer to be executed for his crimes. In contrast, the largest prison in the Union was at Point Lookout in Maryland, which housed no more than 20,000, and the worst death rate was at Elmira, where total casualties reached 24 percent.

President Andrew Johnson.

THE GRAND REVIEW MAY 23 AND 24, 1865

Although there had been earlier celebrations of victory prior to Lincoln's assassination, with new President Andrew Johnson declaring on May 10 that military action was "virtually at an end," it was decided to hold a Grand Review in Washington on May 23 and 24, 1865. The two great Union armies—that of Sherman and General Meade's Army of the Potomac—were to march through the federal capital; Meade's army on the 23rd and Sherman's on the following day. In the period prior to the review, both armies reached Washington, where they encamped on opposite sides of the Potomac River (although this did not prevent soldiers from both sides engaging in drunken brawls).

On May 23 Meade led his army—the more popular locally as it had represented the army tasked with defending Washington—from Capitol Hill, down Pennsylvania Avenue, and past the massed crowds. In front of the White House Johnson and Grant took the salute, being joined by Meade as his 80,000 infantrymen marched past 12 abreast. The Army of the Potomac parade also included several hundred artillery pieces and a procession of cavalry, which included General Custer (who, either deliberately or by accident, ended up passing the review stand twice as he lost control of his horse), that stretched for seven miles. The 24th witnessed Sherman's smaller—65,000-strong—army march past in a procession that took six hours. Sherman's force marched with less precision, but more bravado, incorporating as it did livestock captured from the farms of Carolina and Georgia. Sherman was to describe later the experience of the Review as "the happiest and most satisfactory moment of my life." For most of the soldiers involved, the Grand Review represented the end of their military career as the two grand armies were quickly disbanded.

Ruins of the arsenal at Harpers Ferry, W. Va. The physical reconstruction would take time: the political reintegration of the southern states much, much longer.

RECONSTRUCTION

After the war there was a 12-year period during which the ex-Confederate states were occupied by Federal soldiers while the politicians in Washington endeavored to restore political stability and reintegrate the southern states into the Union. There were issues over civil rights and citizenship, for example, over the freedmen.

As early as December 8, 1863, Lincoln issued a Proclamation of Amnesty and Reconstruction. This outlined ways in which the Confederate states could be reintegrated but at the time was more a means of trying to divide opinion in the South. However, Lincoln's death removed his experience from the thorny issue of reconstruction and bequeathed the pivotal role to his successor, Andrew Johnson of Tennessee. Johnson was a Democrat and had been the only Southern Senator to back the Union in 1861.

Although a Democrat, Johnson was backed by the Republicans and he had, therefore, the potential to act as a bridge between the reformers in the north and the defeated southerners. In this, however, he was to prove a disappointment. While he accepted the 13th Amendment, he believed that there should be no more positive action in furtherance of black rights. Given that the new Congress was not due to meet until December 1865, Johnson had the opportunity to carry out the policy of reconstruction as defined in his Proclamation of Reconstruction of May 29, 1865. This policy allowed considerable freedom to the Southern states and resulted in them passing the so-called "Black Codes," which effectively resulted in slavery in all but name and which were later to be nullified by the Federal military commanders in each of the states concerned.

Engraving of O.S.B. Wall, a recruiter of African-American troops in Ohio during the Civil War, Captain with the 104th U.S. Colored Infantry Regiment and Quartermaster in the Bureau for Freedmen, Refugees, and Abandoned Lands at Charleston, South Carolina.

It was not only by law that the Southern states sought to maintain their position; violence was also rife. The Ku Klux Klan was established at Pulaski, Tennessee, on December 24, 1865, and there were many examples of attacks against blacks of which the most infamous were the race riots of Memphis (April 1866 in which 46 were killed) and the New Orleans Massacre of July 30, 1866. Johnson did little to counter these trends but, from December 1865 when the new Congress met, his position was weakened. On December 4, 1865, Congress established a Joint Committee on Reconstruction. Three important measures were passed by Congress during this period: the 14th Amendment to the Constitution (which included equal protection under the law for all citizens); and extension to the life of the Bureau of Freedmen, Refugees, and Abandoned Lands (a body established prior to the end of the war to aid reconstruction and which was to survive until 1872 when opposition led to its demise); and a Civil Rights Act, which enshrined the citizen rights espoused in the 14th Amendment into law. Johnson sought to veto the various measures, thus starting a conflict with Congress that was ultimately to lead to a campaign for his impeachment, a campaign that failed by a single vote in May 1868.

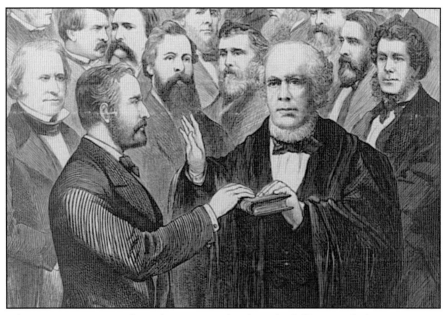

The Inauguration—President Ulysses Grant takes the oath of office, March 4, 1873.

The effect of the race riots in the south was to undermine Johnson and his backers, the so-called Redeemers, and resulted in the Republicans gaining strength in the 1866 Congressional elections. This led to a period known as Radical Reconstruction, with all the southern states—with the exception of Tennessee—being placed under military control while the individual states began the process of political reconstruction. By 1868 only four states—Georgia, Mississippi, Texas, and Virginia—had failed to complete the process and by 1870 all had reconstructed.

Political reconstruction was one part of the process; economic and social reconstruction was the other, and in this, despite the Reconstruction Acts of 1867/68, Congress was less successful. This was partly the consequence of the dire economic condition of the South after the end of the war, and partly an unwillingness, except on the part of the most radical Republicans, to undertake determined action.

In 1868, Johnson lost the Presidency to Ulysses S. Grant, the ex-Union general, who had been backed by the Republicans; there was now greater unity between the President and Congress although it did not result in major reforms. In 1876, Grant lost the Presidential election to Rutherford Hayes. Although there were accusations of fraud, Hayes' election saw the Democrats return to the White House and was a reaction, particularly among Southern voters, to the corruption perceived among many of the Republican administrators that had migrated to the south—the so-called "Carpet Baggers." This paved the way to the Compromise of 1877—a commitment to end reconstruction that resulted in the final withdrawal of the postwar military occupation. However, the compromise effectively enshrined white supremacy in the Southern states, something it would take more than a century to confront.

Sherman's Grand Army. Looking up Pennsylvania Avenue from the Treasury Buildings, Maj. Gen. Logan and staff and Army of Tennessee passing in review.

DECORATION DAY/MEMORIAL DAY

Officially May 30, Memorial Day is celebrated on the last monday of May, although there is pressure for the restoration of the historic date to the calendar. The origins of the day are shrouded in some mystery, with more than 20 towns and cities laying claim to be the first to have marked the loss of life: Waterloo, New York, was officially marked by President Lyndon B. Johnson as the birthplace in May 1966. It would appear that, even before the war had finished, women's groups in the south were decorating the graves of those who had fallen in the war. It is probable that a number of towns and cities marked the loss of life before the day became officially recognized, the momentum of each individual act of commemoration culminating in the decision to make the date official when, on May 5, 1868, General John Logan, commander of the Grand Army of the Republic, issued his General Order No. 11. The day was first officially observed on May 30, 1868, when flowers were placed on graves at Arlington National Cemetery of both Union and Confederate soldiers—part of the idea behind the commemoration was to encourage postwar reconciliation.

The first state to recognize the holiday officially was New York in 1873: by 1890 all of the former Union states had also adopted the date as a holiday. The ex-Confederate states, however, maintained separate days and it was not until after World War I that the south adopted the policy of marking all American war dead on Memorial Day (although many still retain a separate day, such as April 26 in Alabama) specifically to mark the dead from the Civil War. Memorial Day is celebrated now in virtually all states of the U.S. following on from the National Holiday Act of 1971.

National Memorial Reunion and Peace Jubilee, Vicksburg, Miss., October 16-19, 1917.

MEMORIALS

The American Civil War—the war about slavery—was costly in human terms. During the years of the struggle, some 359,000 soldiers from the Union and some 258,000 men from the Confederacy had died, either in battle or in military hospitals. Countless others had suffered injury—physical and mental—in a war that, statistically speaking, was the bloodiest in U.S. history in terms of the absolute numbers of casualties and in term of the proportion of the U.S. population affected. There were few places within the country that had not suffered personal loss. For the ex-Confederate states, however, memorials became a means by which some form of protest could be perpetuated by a non-violent means. As outlined in the section on Memorial Day, even before the end of the war, the Southerners had adopted forms of mourning and commemoration. Very quickly physical memorials appeared in most major Confederate towns and cities. These invariably took the form of a statue of a boy dressed in gray looking resolutely northward.

INDEX